T0355835

Julian

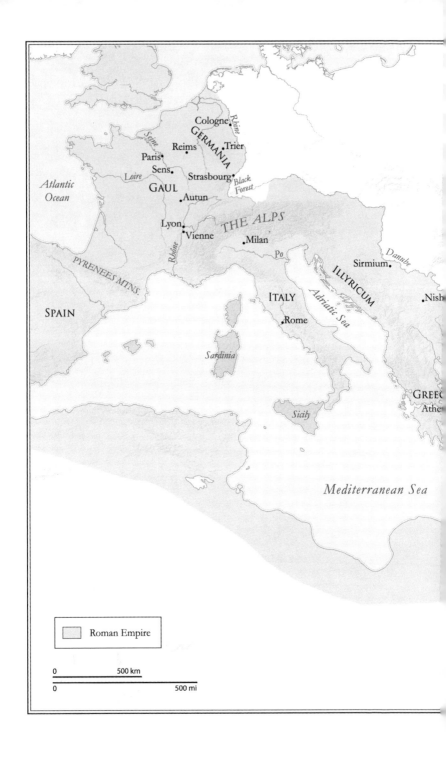

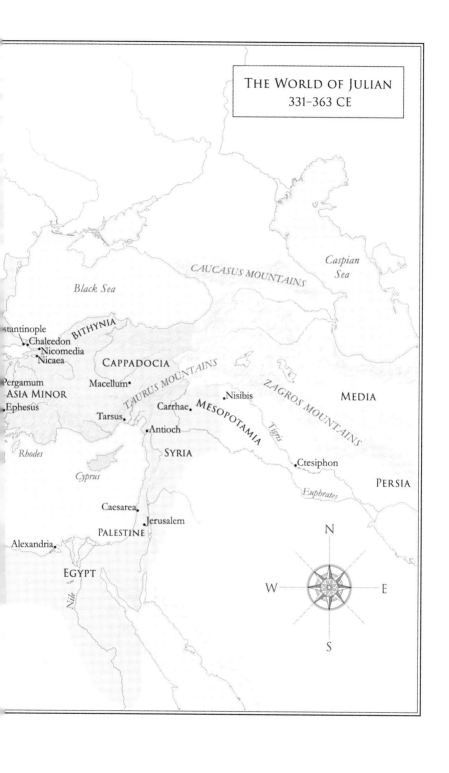

THE WORLD OF JULIAN
331–363 CE

Caspian
Sea

CAUCASUS MOUNTAINS

Black Sea

stantinople
Chalcedon
Nicomedia
BITHYNIA
Nicaea
CAPPADOCIA

Pergamum
Macellum
ASIA MINOR
TAURUS MOUNTAINS
ZAGROS MOUNTAINS
MEDIA
Ephesus
Nisibis
Carrhae
MESOPOTAMIA
Tarsus
Antioch
SYRIA
Tigris
Ctesiphon
Rhodes
PERSIA
Cyprus
Euphrates

Caesarea
Jerusalem
PALESTINE

Alexandria

EGYPT

Nile

N

W   E

S

Julian

Rome's Last Pagan Emperor

Philip Freeman

· ANCIENT LIVES ·

Yale

UNIVERSITY PRESS

NEW HAVEN & LONDON

Published with assistance from the Louis Stern Memorial Fund.

Yale University Press books may be purchased in quantity for
educational, business, or promotional use. For information, please e-mail
sales.press@yale.edu (U.S. office) or sales@yaleup.co.uk (U.K. office).

Frontispiece: Beehive Mapping.

Set in the Yale typeface designed by Matthew Carter, and Louize,
designed by Matthieu Cortat, by Integrated Publishing Solutions.
Printed in the United States of America.

Library of Congress Control Number: 2022950972
ISBN 978-0-300-25664-2 (hardcover : alk. paper)

A catalogue record for this book is available from the British Library.

This paper meets the requirements of ANSI/NISO Z39.48-1992
(Permanence of Paper).

10 9 8 7 6 5 4 3 2 1

· ANCIENT LIVES ·

Ancient Lives unfolds the stories of thinkers, writers, kings, queens, conquerors, and politicians from all parts of the ancient world. Readers will come to know these figures in fully human dimensions, complete with foibles and flaws, and will see that the issues they faced — political conflicts, constraints based in gender or race, tensions between the private and public self — have changed very little over the course of millennia.

James Romm
Series Editor

Contents

Julian

Prologue

A cold wind was blowing fiercely down from the mountains that late November in the year 361 when two towering Germans marched unexpectedly into the palace at Nish where the rebellious young Caesar (the title of a junior emperor) was plotting his next move against the ruler of the Roman Empire. Julian hated the rough-hewn city near the wild Danube frontier far from the "cultured" cities of Greece where he felt most at home. But the fortified town was the key to guarding the borders against the "barbarian" (Frankish and Germanic) tribes of the north that had threatened the empire since the days of the great Augustus more than three centuries earlier. It was also the fastest road for his journey from his assigned province of Gaul through the Balkans and over the Succi Pass before arrival at Constantinople, the new and thriving capital of the greatest empire the Mediterranean world had ever known. But Julian hated Nish most of all because it was forever celebrated as the birthplace of his uncle Constantine the Great. He could scarcely go anywhere in the town without seeing some statue dedicated to the man who had dared deny the ancient gods of Greece and Rome and embrace the cult of a Jewish carpenter and his rag-tag band of Galilean fishermen — a religion, in the opinion of Julian, though himself raised as a faithful Christian, fit only for slaves and fools. Needless to say, as a member of a the most powerful Christian family in the world, he had kept his beliefs to himself.

The two German soldiers who appeared before him surrounded by imperial guards that day were named Theolaifus and Aligildus, known to Julian as loyal senior officers of his enemy and cousin Constantius. They caused Julian no alarm, as he had commanded and fought against such men for the past few years in Gaul in the service of the emperor. Julian had been sent with the title of Caesar to the western edge of the empire to fly the imperial flag and show the populace that their emperor supposedly cared so deeply for their safety that he was placing his own kinsmen among them to protect them against the fierce Germans from across the Rhine. Never mind that half the soldiers and officers in the Roman legions of Gaul were themselves Germans who fought for gold against their relatives across the river. Constantius did not bother to note that Julian was just a philosophy student in his early twenties who knew about battles only from books. The important thing in the eyes of the emperor was that his cousin was a member of the royal family and so a visible reminder to the Gauls of their faraway emperor's love for them. And of course no one at court mentioned that Julian was chosen because Constantius had murdered everyone else he was related to by blood, including Julian's father and brother. But Julian was full of surprises. A natural general and leader of men, he had driven back the Germans and proven such a success that his own men had proclaimed him co-emperor with Constantius while he was busy fighting the Persians on the eastern frontier. Julian's tepid denials that he had ever wanted such equal standing did not impress his older cousin, so the two were now marching from opposite directions across the empire toward civil war — though few wagered on the success of Julian against the vastly larger army, greater experience, and utter ruthlessness of Constantius.

It was thus a shock when the two Germans, clearly exhausted from days of hard riding, fell to their knees before Julian and held up a golden crown. The story they told was even more surprising. They had been with Constantius fighting on the Persian frontier when the emperor had driven back their forces and forged an uneasy peace in order to turn his attention to his treacherous Caesar in the West. His goal was to race Julian to Constantinople and crush him before he could approach the capital. He had marched his veteran soldiers quickly through the city of Antioch and then quickly on to Tarsus, birthplace of the Christian apostle Paul. But the omens were troubling, even for a Christian such as Constantius — for example, when he saw a headless man on the road outside Tarsus stretched out toward the west, he was unsure whether the man foretold the fate of himself or of Julian. At Tarsus, Constantius pressed on, even when he came down with a mild fever. Upward through the mountains of Cilicia he continued until he soon fell deathly ill at the base of the snow-covered Taurus Mountains. His body grew so hot it could not be touched, while remedies applied by the finest physicians proved useless. Knowing that he had little time left, Constantius asked for a deathbed baptism to wash away his sins at the last moments of life. The two Germans swore that his final words had been to declare Julian his legitimate successor. The former philosophy student and secret pagan, only thirty years of age and the last surviving relative of the holy Christian emperor Constantine the Great, was now the sole ruler of the Roman Empire.

Few figures from ancient times have captured the modern imagination like Flavius Claudius Julianus, better known as Julian the

Apostate. He ruled Rome for just over a year and a half, but during that short span he threatened to turn the world upside down. Although a nephew of the first Christian emperor of Rome, Julian soon openly abandoned his family's faith and fought to return Rome to the old gods, who had led his ancestors to build one of the greatest empires the world had ever known. His efforts ultimately failed, but for almost seventeen hundred years his admirers have seen him as a tragic and quixotic figure, a lonely hero raging against the dying light of pagan civilization. Christian writers and historians from his own time forward have seen Julian in a very different way, as a traitor to God and violent oppressor of those who followed the true faith.

Like most famous people from history, Julian was neither as ideal as his supporters would have us believe nor as monstrous as his enemies portray him. He was above all a complicated man who in his short reign blazed like a comet across the sky of Late Antiquity. That he failed in his efforts to hold back the inrushing tide of Christianity is not surprising, but his lack of success should not distract us from his remarkable accomplishments as a skilled general, masterful administrator, and gifted writer. If not for a lucky Persian (or was it Roman?) spear on a distant battlefield, Julian might have ruled the empire for decades and accomplished everything he set out to do. But we would be living in a very different world from the one we know today.

How can we form an accurate picture of such a controversial man, who lived so long ago? As it happens, in contrast to the paucity of sources for many key figures of late Roman times, an abundance of documentation survives for the short life of Julian, including the writings of Julian himself, detailed descriptions of the emperor by his friends and enemies, preserved legal decrees, contemporary inscriptions, and even coinage minted under him. But as is so often the case in shaping the story of a person from the past, each of these sources must be approached with caution, and none can be trusted completely.

The surviving letters, satires, hymns, and other works composed by Julian are of the greatest importance and constitute a key resource for understanding the life and mind of the emperor. Few figures from antiquity apart from Cicero give us a clearer view of both their public and their private lives in their writings. Some of these compositions, such as Julian's gushing panegyric praising the emperor Constantius, were formulaic works that were never meant to be read as sincere, but they nonetheless provide a great deal of biographical information about Julian's early life as he struggled to survive in the violent world of the Roman imperial court. His letters to Athens and other Greek cities in which he tried to justify his revolt against Constantius are more revealing about his true feelings, as well as his motives for civil war. His *Misopogon* (Beard-Hater) is a scolding attack on the "ungrateful" people of Antioch disguised as a self-satire that reveals Julian in one of his worst moments as a prickly ruler who has lost his patience with an entire city. The full text of his powerful anti-Christian tract *Against the Galileans* was lost in antiquity, but much was preserved in extensive quotations within an early Christian response by Cyril of Alexandria. Two of Julian's hymns to the gods, however, did survive the centuries and reveal a person of deep religious faith and spiritual sensibility. But it is unsurprisingly in his personal letters that we are able to see most clearly the private Julian, with all his strengths and weaknesses. They are a treasure for any biographer. Taken as a whole, the writings of Julian are of tremendous value since they present an amazingly clear portrait of the man—though as with any of us, authors are not always the truest sources or most balanced critics of their own lives.

Two of the best contemporary commentators on his life are a sympathetic pagan professor and a hostile Christian bishop, both of whom knew him personally. Libanius, from the Greek city of Antioch in Syria, was a celebrated teacher of rhetoric and a prominent public figure, respected across the religious spectrum. He became a friend and ardent supporter of Julian, composing among other works a funeral oration for the emperor that gives us a detailed outline of his life and goals. Libanius is a faithful presenter of the facts about Julian and trustworthy in his information but deliberately selective, and careful to include only the flattering aspects of his career. Equally informative, though holding very different religious views, Gregory of Nazianzus in Cappadocia was a schoolmate of Julian's in Athens and later an influential Christian bishop. Although a faithful Christian, he was deeply immersed in the Hellenic literary and philosophical tradition he shared with the emperor. His writings on his former friend are passionately antagonistic but generally reliable in their details about his life.

One of the most promising sources for the life of Julian is the detailed history of Ammianus Marcellinus, a native of Antioch who nonetheless wrote in Latin and became the last of the great Roman historians. Ammianus was a career military officer who served in Gaul when Julian was a mere Caesar and later participated in the emperor's disastrous invasion of Persia, though he was never personally close to him. He was a confirmed pagan, a measured opponent of Christianity, and an admirer of Julian, though unafraid to criticize the excesses of the emperor's campaign to restore traditional Roman religion. His balanced, year-by-year account of the reign of Julian would seem an ideal source for discovering his story, and indeed is invaluable, but Ammianus composed his history decades after Julian's death, often from secondary sources, and was sometimes more interested in style than substance. Nonetheless, the account of Ammianus is crucial for forming an accurate picture of Julian.

Other ancient accounts are also valuable, such as the now lost history of the pagan writer Eunapius, who drew on another lost work by Julian's closest friend and physician, Oribasius. Eunapius was often paraphrased by the late-fifth-century Greek historian Zosimus in his own work, portions of which do survive. Later Christian writers, such as Ephrem of Nisbis, who reviled Julian, nonetheless preserve some valuable information about him and give a crucial Christian perspective to his actions. Other later writers had access to works about Julian we no longer possess and can be useful to our understanding of the emperor. Remaining sources which are helpful for forming a clearer picture of Julian include the Theodosian Code, which contains the texts of imperial decrees issued by Julian, along with inscriptions carved at the time of the emperor and coins, often an important medium for imperial propaganda. All in all, we have abundant yet at times frustratingly contradictory sources for a biography of Julian. Weighing them all carefully and arriving at the clearest picture we can is the challenge faced by historians and readers alike. But when we make the effort, we can discover one of the most fascinating people in history.

CHAPTER ONE

A Cross in the Sky

Julian was born in the year 331 into an ambitious, murderous, and thoroughly Christian family. The city of his birth was Constantinople, founded a few years earlier as the new Roman capital by his uncle Constantine and dedicated to the glory of Jesus Christ. The fact that Julian as emperor would become one of the greatest enemies the church had ever known would have shocked his family—if any of them had survived long enough to see him take the throne.

No one would have been more disappointed and angrier at Julian than Constantine himself, the man who two decades before his nephew's birth had become the first Christian emperor of Rome. Constantine's embrace of the new faith had profound implications for the future of the empire, all the more because Christianity was still a divided and struggling sect that had won over no more than a small minority of the population in the three centuries since it had been established in a poor and troubled corner of the Roman world.

The Romans always had a grudging respect for the Jews because of their ancient traditions and disciplined morality. However, this did not stop Roman legions from making war on the Jews and enforcing a harsh and brutal peace in Palestine. Violence was commonplace, and rebellion against Roman authority was met with a swift and merciless response. It was in this troubled land that Yeshua bar Yosef, known later as Jesus, conducted his brief ministry as a traveling rabbi and healer. When he was crucified in Jerusalem under the Roman governor Pontius Pilate during the reign of the emperor Tiberius, he was dismissed as yet another rebel who would soon be forgotten. But to the small group of his Jewish followers who claimed he had risen from the dead, he was divine. Starting in Jerusalem, they spread their new religion, which grew and was soon embraced by non-Jews through the efforts of wandering missionaries such as Paul of Tarsus who established communities of Christians in towns and cities around the Mediterranean and beyond. The followers of Jesus met in the homes of the few wealthy members of local congregations for fellowship, instruction, and a sacred meal, practices that reflected a pattern common to many religious groups of the time. But unlike adherents of many other sacred organizations, the Christians were known for welcoming women and slaves into their community, as well as for their acts of public, universal charity in a world in which the untended poor routinely starved to death.

But Christians soon ran into trouble with the government for their refusal to sacrifice to the emperor and the gods of Rome. This was not a spiritual failing in the eyes of the Romans, who tended to be tolerant of religious differences among their subjects, but an act of civic rebellion against the emperor that threatened the harmony of the larger community. The failure to sacrifice to the emperor was tantamount to rejecting the authority that held civilization together in a hostile world. In the early second century, Pliny the Younger, who was serving as Roman governor of Bithynia in

Asia Minor, wrote to his friend the emperor Trajan for advice on how to punish Christians brought before him on trial for impiety. Trajan's response set the tone for Roman officials for the next two centuries: "The Christians are not to be sought out by the authorities. However, if they are denounced and proven guilty they should be punished. But whoever who is willing to deny publicly that he is a Christian and proves it by worshipping our gods, even though he was under suspicion in the past, shall be pardoned because of his repentance."[1]

For the most part Christians were allowed to live in peace throughout the empire even if they did not sacrifice to the gods. Persecution was sporadic and often initiated locally by a few zealous governors hoping to impress the emperor with their diligence, rather than by any broad mandate from Rome. There were notable Christian martyrs from time to time in Gaul, Asia Minor, Africa, and Rome itself, but the followers of Jesus were generally permitted to worship their God without interference. As Christianity was one of many competing cults in the great marketplace of religious pluralism that was the Roman Empire, officials tended to ignore them as long as they were discreet and paid their taxes. The Christian communities, for their part, went about quiet lives, led by their local bishops and welcoming anyone who was interested into their fellowship.

It was the crisis of the third century that set the stage for the revolution that was to come. Throughout that long and painful century Rome was beset by countless problems — including invasions by foreign tribes, plague and other diseases, economic collapse, and endless imperial coups and rebellions — that almost destroyed the empire. Some rulers sought to restore the stability of Rome by enforcing uniformity of religion among their citizens. The emperor Decius in 250 ordered everyone in the Roman Empire to sacrifice to the gods in front of a panel of local officials and receive a certificate for doing so. Many of the Christians who refused were punished or even executed, though with the ascension of a new emperor a decade later the rules were eased.

The rise of the emperor Diocletian at the end of the third century brought about the last and fiercest of the persecutions against the Christians. Diocletian was not by nature cruel or a fanatically religious person, but he was passionately dedicated to restoring Rome to its former glory. One way he attempted this was to divide the governance of the empire between two senior rulers, called Augusti, and two junior rulers, known as Caesars, with himself as the dominant Augustus. His hope was that the Caesars would smoothly step into the role of senior emperors when the Augusti retired. He also transformed the court of the emperor by adding elaborate, Persian-style ceremonies to elevate the sovereign far above the common people and instill awe in his subjects. But his most notable reform was to firmly suppress any religious movement that he saw as a threat to the traditional values and gods that had made Rome great. First among these supposedly dangerous cults was Manichaeanism, a Persian import with adherents throughout the empire. But he also took aim at the Christians and issued edicts to burn their scriptures, demolish their places of assembly, and ban their worship services. He renewed the earlier demand for universal sacrifice to the gods as proof of loyalty. Declared Christians of free birth in the imperial service were stripped of rank, and those who were freedmen were returned to slavery. But not all of Diocletian's fellow rulers shared his interest in hunting down Christians. The Caesar for the far west of the empire, a practical general named Flavius Valerius Constantius, contented himself with knocking down a few churches. As always, most of the anti-Christian persecutions took place in the more populated, richer, eastern part of the realm, where Christianity had spread more widely.

Aside from having little interest in religious persecution, Constantius, later known as Chlorus, was far too busy trying to hold Britain and Gaul for the empire to waste military resources on hunting down Christians. The Germans across the Rhine were a constant threat to Gaul, and Saxon raiders were repeatedly attacking the coast of Britain, while Picts and Scots descended on the Romans across Hadrian's Wall from the north and from Ireland to the west. Constantius spent much of his time in the walled city of York, the northernmost town of the Roman Empire, coordinating the defense of the island, while his fellow rulers denied him the resources he needed for fear he might lead his army south or east against them.

Early in his career Constantius Chlorus had married a common innkeeper named Helena, who bore him a son, Constantine, but when he rose in power he divorced Helena and took Theodora, a woman of the nobility, as his new wife. Theodora in turn gave birth to a son named Julius Constantius, who got along well enough with his older half-brother Constantine. Five other children from Theodora added to the rapidly growing family. The tangle of stepparents and half-siblings may have made the relations of Constantius Chlorus hard for the common people to keep straight, but it was a typical blended family of the Roman upper class, whose male members were usually willing to give up one wife if a better-connected woman came along. But for the coming years at least, the ties of loyalty among the children and grandchildren – including Julian – of Constantius Chlorus and the need for unity against outside threats would keep at bay the murderous infighting endemic to Roman ruling families that stretched back to Romulus slaying his brother Remus.

———

Constantine, the eldest son of Constantius Chlorus, was born in the town of Nish in the Balkans not far from the turbulent border of the empire. When his father was chosen by Diocletian as Caesar for Gaul and Britain, the twenty-one-year-old Constantine remained behind in the service of Diocletian as a military tribune and hostage for the good behavior of his father. He was a skilled soldier and fought enthusiastically on battlefields across the empire from Persia to the Danube. Contrary to all expectations, Diocletian retired peacefully from his role as senior emperor in 305 and handed the office of dual Augusti to his Caesars Galerius in the East as senior Augustus and Constantius as his junior in the West, after forcing his fellow Augustus, Maximian, to retire as well. Before Galerius could find an excuse to hold him, Constantine left for Britain to help his father defend the island against the Picts. Constantine was thus present at York the next year, when his father, Constantius, suddenly died. The legions in Britain had admired Constantius as a good general and saw the same qualities in his son. Though he was only in his early thirties, the troops proclaimed him as Augustus, an act that in the past that had often led to civil war. Galerius, the senior Augustus ruling in the East, was occupied by other problems and contented himself with a stern rebuke, recognizing young Constantine as Caesar only, and giving the title of Augustus in the West to his comrade Severus.

Constantine spent the next few years based at the key Roman fortress of Trier on the Rhine border between Gaul and Germany. He honed his skills as a general and administrator while building a network of supporters throughout the empire for the fight for power and survival he knew would soon come. Only a year after taking office as Augustus in the West, Galerius's ally Severus was overthrown and executed by Maxentius (the son of the previous emperor, Maximian), who claimed the title of Augustus for himself in Rome. He also invited his father to join him, shattering the fragile system of succession that Diocletian had established. Galerius invaded Italy to drive Maxentius out, but failed, instead appointing a comrade named Licinius as a rival Augustus, along with a general named Maximinus. Maximian soon eclipsed his son in Italy, and he strengthened his position further when he made an alliance with Constantine, naming him Augustus in Gaul and giving him his daughter Fausta in marriage. Maxentius in turn then drove his overbearing father out of Italy, forcing Maximian to find shelter with Constantine at his Gaulish court. By this point even the most informed citizens across the empire were having trouble keeping track of who was in charge.

Constantine spent the next few years defending the Rhine frontier and quarreling with Galerius but managing to avoid an outright civil war. He fought bravely against the Franks and bridged the Rhine to launch punishing raids into Germany. In 310, while he was fighting the Germans, Constantine received reports that his ally, the former emperor Maximian, was trying to regain power, prompting Constantine to turn on him and force him to commit suicide. When Galerius died the next year, his protégés Maximinus and Licinius barely avoided civil war by dividing the empire between themselves, leaving Constantine temporarily marginalized but willing to make an alliance with Licinius against Maximinus.

In 312, when Constantine was thirty-nine, he finally made his move. With the consent of Licinius he invaded Italy and successfully faced the forces of Maximinus in the Po Valley before moving on to Rome. There in late October, at a place known as Saxa Rubra just north of the city, he met Maximinus, defeating and killing his rival at the Milvian Bridge over the Tiber River. Under pressure from Constantine, the Senate in Rome prudently recognized his new standing and officially named him as Augustus. With Britain, Gaul, Spain, Italy, and Africa under his rule, Constantine became the most powerful man in the western Roman Empire.

It was at the Milvian Bridge that, according to later stories, a miracle occurred. Constantine had never been an especially religious man, but like many Romans, and particularly those in the army, he paid homage to Sol Invictus, the unconquered sun, often merged in worship with the god Apollo. Many Christians saw the sun as a symbol of Christ, though their bishops repeatedly warned them not to confuse the celestial creation of God with the creator. Roman generals were forever declaring visions of victory to their men on the eve of battle to boost their morale. In the past Constantine had told his army that he had seen the sun god Apollo and the goddess Victory along with the symbol "XXX" to indicate the thirty years of rule the god had granted him. Before the conflict at the Milvian Bridge he reported to his soldiers that he had a dream in which he was told that his men should put a cross on their shields. This could have been the Chi-Rho (☧) symbol from the first two letters of the name of Christ in Greek, though it might as easily have been the start of the Greek word *chrestos* (luck). There is no indication in the earliest sources on the battle that the symbol was intended to be a Christian cross, but by the time Constantine was an old man the story had evolved into a tale worthy of Saint Paul's conversion on the road to Damascus. The famous Arch of Constantine in the Roman Forum, dedicated three years after the Milvian Bridge battle, tellingly has no Christian images and bears only a vague inscription stating that Constantine was "inspired by the divine" in his victory. Even his coins minted ten years after the battle were still decorated with images of the god Sol Invictus.

Whoever Constantine believed inspired his victory that day outside Rome, he nonetheless experienced a gradual but genuine change of heart and mind from that point forward. He began to look favorably on the Christian God, though he by no means abandoned the other gods of Rome. A cynic might see Constantine's conversion experience in purely political terms, but there was no reason for the practical benefits of embracing Christianity to exclude a sincere and growing faith. Even so, Constantine was a consummate player in the game of Roman politics and was never above using and manipulating the church to enhance his power throughout his life.

Although Christians made up a small minority of the Roman population, Constantine believed they could be useful to his career. The empire had long embraced countless polytheistic religions, but in recent decades a shift to an increasingly monotheistic view had taken place among many of Rome's pagan thinkers, as well as among the common people. This idea of a single God was reflected in the cult of Sol Invictus and other religious and philosophical expressions, but it lacked the focus and theology found in Judaism and Christianity. The ritual requirements and uncomfortable foreignness of Judaism ruled out that religion as an option for many Romans, but Christianity, with its easy entry and simple teachings, held a growing appeal among a variety of classes. Constantine also knew that Christians had a constantly quarreling but generally effective organization that stretched across the empire and could help bring the discordant Roman world together. Although several of the different Christian groups would barely talk to each other and disagreed on even minor doctrinal issues, if with the backing and authority of a ruling Roman emperor they could be molded into a single, unified church, they would be a powerful ally indeed.

In February 313, Constantine began the elevation of Christianity by issuing a joint document, known as the Edict of Milan, with his co-emperor Licinius, officially declaring religious freedom in the Roman Empire from that day forward. Christians and other religious groups would be allowed to worship as they pleased if they caused no trouble. Constantine also began restoring property that had been seized from believers during the previous persecutions. He then granted special privileges to the Christian clergy, such as exemptions from civil service and the right to use the imperial transport at no cost. He also began to construct at state expense churches for local communities, beginning with the bishop and Christians of the city of Rome. Across the Tiber River on the Vatican Hill a church rose above the burial place of the apostle Peter, dedicated to the saint, who had died there. Constantine's architectural model for such buildings was not the ancient temple of the gods but the more practical Roman basilica, a civic gathering place found in every major town, which allowed large crowds of Christians to worship openly for the first time in their history. For a persecuted group accustomed to small, secret meetings in homes, these changes represented a heady and sudden change in status. Many pagan intellectuals and working people throughout the empire grumbled at the use of public tax money to favor a minority religious cult, but the emperor was the emperor. Ambitious government officials and ministers of the imperial court either quickly discovered a new-found interest in Christianity or learned to keep quiet and practice their sacrifices discreetly.

Constantine had taken a big risk in backing Christianity, and it was imperative that the church give him good value in return. To profit from his alliance with Christians he needed them to form a united front behind him, but they were a contentious collection of factions, each convinced it was the only true representative of Jesus on earth. One group centered in North Africa posed particular difficulties for Constantine throughout his reign. During the wave of previous persecutions many Christians had publicly denounced their faith to save their lives and those of their families, but now they returned to the church repentant, declaring that they had never been sincere in abandoning God. Those Christians, called Donatists, who had stood firm and refused to renounce their religion in spite of the consequences considered these apostates false Christians and themselves to be the only true church. Both sides appealed to Constantine to give imperial recognition to their claims regarding church property and clerical standing. Constantine responded that they must resolve the matter since he put Christian cooperation above petty squabbles and feared God would remove him from the throne if he could not bring about unity in the church. When this tactic failed, he resorted to threats and occasional executions to try to reconcile the two sides, but it took more than a century for the conflict to be resolved in favor of those in opposition to the unyielding Donatists.

A more pressing problem for Constantine was unifying Christians throughout the empire in a single belief system. For three hundred years the followers of Jesus had been divided into countless sects that held differing theological views. Sometimes these divergent views were minor, such as the question of when to celebrate a particular holy day, but many were much larger and deeply divisive, such as the structure of church authority or the nature of Christ. One such group of Christians, led by the cleric Arius, taught that Jesus was created by God and thus subordinate to the Father. These Christians, known later as Arians, were not much different in other theological respects from the more orthodox strain of Christians promoted by Athanasius, who would become bishop of Alexandria — but no religious contention is as bitter as that between similar groups. The Arians made up a large portion of Christians in the empire and could not be ignored. They were also more successful in their missionary work beyond the frontiers, converting many tribes in Germany and the Balkans.

Constantine tried his best to gently reconcile the Arians, orthodox, and other Christian groups, but in the end he abandoned subtlety and called the first ever universal council of Christian bishops to gather together and hammer out a short and simple creed stating clearly what all good Christians were required to believe. It was a very practical Roman solution to an esoteric problem. Constantine summoned the council to the town of Nicaea in northwest Asia Minor in 325 and oversaw the proceedings himself. The emperor flattered, threatened, and bullied the attendees into working out an accord. The bishops could agree for the most part on the nature of God, the Holy Spirit, the unity of the church, and the resurrection of the dead, but they could not find common ground on the nature of Jesus. What exactly did it mean for him to be the Son of God? Was he created by God at some point in time or was he co-equal with God from the beginning of the universe? The Arians favored Christ as subordinate to God the Father, but the orthodox were willing to bring the whole gathering crashing down if they could not get their way. In the end Constantine forced the council to accept the orthodox position, though with compromises that left everyone unhappy. But the emperor got his document of Christian unity, and that was what mattered to him.

At almost the same time as the Council of Nicaea, Constantine founded the city of Constantinople as the new capital of the Roman Empire on the site of the ancient city of Byzantium at the entrance to the Black Sea. It was both a practical and a symbolic move on the part of the emperor. The economic and population center of gravity in the empire had been shifting east away from Italy for centuries. The new foundation also allowed the government to be based closer to potential threats from Persia or from across the Danube to the north. But to Constantine it was also an opportunity to begin with a clean slate and establish a Christian city on a hill as a shining example to the world. It would become a capital of churches without any new temples to the gods, although those already in the city were quietly left in place. Chief among the shrines to martyrs and Christian basilicas throughout the city was the Church of the Holy Apostles, where Constantine's family would henceforth be buried as a symbol to all of their unshakable faith.

Constantine's relatives realized the necessity of supporting the religion of their family's leader. His mother, Helena, the divorced former innkeeper and future saint, now promoted to the rank of Augusta, became an enthusiastic Christian pilgrim and traveled throughout Palestine founding churches and collecting holy relicts. His sons Constantine II, Constantius, and Constans also adopted the Christian faith of their father, though they tended toward the Arian variety. All Constantine's relatives realized that it was essential to present a united front to the Roman world as a Christian family without any dissension that Constantine's enemies might use to weaken their hold on power. Whether they took to heart the teachings of Jesus on kindness and mercy was less to the point.

In 337 Constantine knew that he was dying and received baptism at last, a common postponement in the ancient world to ensure that sins were washed away before death. When he died he had the consolation of knowing he had ruled Rome longer than any emperor since the first Augustus more than three hundred years earlier. This long reign gave him time to firmly establish his family's control over the empire and to secure the central place of Christianity in the Roman world. That world still held many more pagans than Christians, but it was clear that in time the new faith would become dominant with the support of the government and Constantine's heirs, whose fates were now bound firmly to Christianity. The imperial family knew that whatever challenges lay ahead and whatever steps they might have to take to maintain power over the Roman Empire, the one rule they could not break was unswerving loyalty to the religion of Constantine.

CHAPTER TWO

The Early Years

Julian was only six years old when his uncle Constantine died. After this, as the orator Libanius later described, the palace was a dangerous place: "Murder stalked the whole family, both fathers and sons."[1]

The late emperor had intended his three grown sons — Julian's cousins Constantine II, Constantius, and Constans — to rule the empire amicably together in Christian harmony, but that was not how things worked out. The three brothers divided the empire between them and set out to rule as Augusti, but soon Constantine II perished in a battle against the army of Constans. The victorious Constans himself died ten years later when he was overthrown and murdered by a Gaulish usurper named Magnentius, who had accused Constans of excessive cruelty. This left the clever and patient Constantius, a confirmed Christian, to defeat Magnentius and ascend to the throne as the sole ruler of the empire. By this point Constantius had no rivals, for he had long since killed any other family members who might have posed a threat. His father Constantine's half-brother Julius Constantius — Julian's father and a former consul who had served the emperor faithfully for years — stood ready to serve Constantine's son loyally as well, but his blood was too royal for Constantius's comfort. While church leaders turned their heads, Constantius had Julius and eight of his close relatives murdered to prevent them from challenging him. In the bloody aftermath, no one was left alive among the family of Constantine the Great to threaten Constantius. The only exceptions were the two sons of Julius Constantius, Julian and his older half-brother, Gallus, both mere boys. Even Constantius blanched at shedding the blood of young children. Julian, however, would never forget the vicious hypocrisy of the supposedly Christian emperor who had exterminated his entire family.

Julian's mother, Basilina, was born into an old and noble Greek family in Bithynia in Asia Minor, not far east of Constantinople. We know very little about her except that she came from a Christian family of wealth and property, and her father, Julianus, had served as an important Roman administrator under Constantine. She had at least one sister, who bore a son named Procopius, a cousin of Julian's who after Julian's death would try (and fail) to take advantage of his tenuous royal connection to overthrow the emperor Valens. Basilina received an excellent education under a tutor named Mardonius, who would also become an important figure in Julian's young life. She was betrothed in a marriage of political alliance to Julian's father. Her new husband was older than she and had been married previously to a woman named Galla, who had given birth to Gallus, Julian's half-brother. Basilina and her new husband left the quiet country life of Bithynia for the lively capital of Constantinople but had scarce time to enjoy the city. Just a few months after giving birth to her only child, Basilina died, and her son grew up knowing her only through stories. This separation from women would be a common theme in Julian's life as a man who had little knowledge of, and few close relationships with, the opposite sex.

Now Julian had neither mother nor father to guide and comfort him as a young boy in a dangerous and unpredictable world. He was soon sent away from his home in Constantinople to a lonely life in the care of his maternal grandmother on her country estate in Bithynia. There he was under the spiritual guardianship of Bishop Eusebius of nearby Nicomedia, who made sure the boy received a proper religious upbringing. Eusebius belonged to the Arian Christian sect, but so did many in the court of Constantius. Aside from their tedious disagreements with their orthodox brethren regarding the exact place of Christ in the Trinity, the Arians were as Christian as any faithful emperor might wish. Julian spent the most formative years of his childhood studying the holy scriptures with Bishop Eusebius; in his adult life he could still quote much of the Old and New Testaments with ease, often to devastating effect against his Christian adversaries.

Far more important in the life of young Julian than his grandmother or the bishop was his elderly tutor Mardonius, a eunuch from the wild northern lands of Scythia who had been raised and educated as a slave in the household of Julian's maternal grandfather and had tutored Julian's mother as well. From the time Julian was seven, Mardonius was the young orphan's intellectual model, his dearest friend, and the closest thing he would ever have to a father figure. As he wrote later in life, in leaving Mardonius, he dearly missed "the labors we shared and endured together, our honest and candid conversations, our pure and upright companionship, our striving together in everything good, our equally matched and unapologetic zeal to combat evildoers. How often we supported each other with one equal spirit! How alike we were in our ways! How precious was our friendship!"[2]

Mardonius trained the bright and eager young Julian in the greatest writings and ideas of the Greek golden age. If some of his previous students lacked the intelligence and desire to learn from the classics, Julian emphatically did not. The boy enthusiastically devoured Hesiod, Thucydides, Plato, Aristotle, Xenophon, and the rest of Greek literature, especially the poetry of Homer. Mardonius was almost certainly a Christian since it is unlikely the bishop would have allowed the boy a pagan tutor, but the old Scythian seems to have worn his faith lightly — or at least in a fashion that admitted no conflict with the Hellenism he loved and taught. Many of the most devout Christians of the age likewise saw no contradiction between the Gospels and pagan Greek thought. On the contrary, to them Christ was the fulfilment of what the earlier philosophers had been yearning for. Men like Mardonius were able to reconcile with ease the timeless wisdom of Hellenism with the newfound Christian revelations of the Bible. Although Julian must have learned from his tutor that these two worlds were compatible, it may have been at this early age that some of the more glaring contradictions of Christianity and pagan philosophy first began to trouble the soul of the future emperor.

When he was not studying philosophy with Mardonius or sacred scriptures with Eusebius, young Julian would often make his way to the top of a hill on his grandmother's estate from which he could look down on the sparkling blue waters of the Sea of Marmara. Years later he wrote of how he missed that time: "It was very peaceful to lie there and read a book. Then to give my eyes a rest, to gaze at the ships and the distant sea. When I was still hardly more than a boy I thought this was the most delightful place in the summer. It has excellent springs and a pool to bathe in and gardens and trees. When I had grown to be a man I used to long for my old life there and visited it often."[3] Julian would find little peace in his life, but on his childhood hill in Bithynia he was happy.

Julian may have returned to Constantinople with Mardonius at the age of nine, when Eusebius was promoted to bishop of the city, but if so the interlude in the capital did not last long. Constantius had been kept carefully informed of the progress of the upbringing of Julian and his brother Gallus, his only living relatives. From the regular reports he received he knew that the younger boy showed great promise as a scholar, perhaps even as a future bishop, while Gallus had potential as a soldier and administrator. But the fact that he had murdered their father and family was ever present in the emperor's mind. Innocent young boys would grow into men someday and could seek revenge if given a chance. Constantius surely contemplated killing both of his young cousins outright, but he also was aware that he had no other living heirs since he had so far been unable to father a child. The family line of Constantine needed to be preserved to provide continuity of power in the empire. And so the emperor allowed the boys to live, a delicate balance he continued for the next three years, training them as future rulers of Rome while always holding them on a tight leash. He hoped that they could be persuaded to look beyond the death of their father and serve the greater family of Constantine. There might come a time when he would have to have to slit their throats, but not yet.

Although both Julian, now twelve, and his brother Gallus were still too young to be a threat, the emperor was not one to take chances. Constantinople or even Bithynia was too close to the center of imperial power and potential allies for his comfort, so Constantius sent them into exile in a distant corner of the empire. Their place of banishment was a royal estate at Macellum in Cappadocia in central Anatolia, many days' travel from Constantinople. It was a beautiful spot near the thriving town of Caesarea at the foot of a snow-covered volcanic mountain named Argaeus. The estate had a comfortable palace and was famous for its gardens, but it was none-theless a prison. Saddest of all for Julian, he was separated from his old tutor Mardonius, who was forced to stay behind in Constanti-nople. Undoubtably officials at court who were keeping a careful eye on Julian's upbringing wanted to break any bonds that might tie him to his mother's family.

As Julian later wrote, he was not allowed to have friends or to see anyone his own age at Macellum. He complained that he lived as if he were being watched by a garrison of Persian soldiers. He saw Gallus regularly, but the two boys were utterly different in disposition and interests, and Julian seems never to have been close to his brother. Julian's later adversary Gregory of Nazianzus records a story that the two were compelled to practice theological debates together by their tutors at Macellum. Gregory claimed that Julian always took the side of the pagans because he wanted to hone his rhetorical skills by choosing the weaker argument, though Greg-ory's implication is that even at this tender age the boy had pagan tendencies. Gregory also relates that at this time Julian and Gallus rebuilt a chapel dedicated to a Christian saint named Mamas, who had been martyred as a teenager by a Roman emperor in the pre-vious century. In the pious story, the part of the chapel rebuilt by Julian later collapsed in an earthquake while that constructed by Gallus remained standing firm. But in spite of the supposed insight of later church historians, Julian showed no signs of abandoning his Christian faith at this early age. Several years later, however, he does record in a hymn to the god Helios that even as a boy he had an unusual longing for the rays of the sun, seeing its brightness as a metaphor for the growing thirst in his soul for deeper spiritual meaning: "From my childhood an extraordinary longing for the shining rays of the god pierced deep into my soul. From my earliest years my mind was so completely overcome by the light that rules the sky that not only did I desire to gaze at the brightness of the sun, but also whenever I walked on a clear and cloudless night I abandoned all else and gave myself up to the beauty of the heavens."[4] Although the sun was a heavenly symbol commonly used at the time by both pagans and Christians, Julian's tutors cautioned him against inclinations they believed might lead him away from the true teachings of the church.

Julian's only constant companions for the six years he was exiled at Macellum were the slaves who attended him and the surly eunuchs of Constantius assigned to carefully monitor him. Julian spent his teenage years virtually alone, without friends, surrounded by imperial agents who watched his every move. When not spying on him, the eunuchs oversaw his continued instruction in the Christian faith. But Julian had so thoroughly mastered the scriptures and writings of the church fathers that he had soon left his teachers behind. The royal eunuchs were embarrassed that a teenage boy was a far better exponent of the Christian tradition than they were.

In fact, the only true and constant companions of Julian from age twelve to eighteen were books. From his earliest years Julian loved to read, and at Macellum he was allowed access to the large and diverse library of the nearby Bishop George of Cappadocia. It contained plenty of texts on Christian theology, but the collection also had many scrolls on literature, history, philosophy, rhetoric, and pagan religious beliefs. Julian had convinced George, perhaps still sincerely at this point, that he was a true Christian and could be trusted to read works that challenged the teachings of Christianity, if only to be prepared in the future to counter the arguments of the enemy. Julian was so attached to the library of Bishop George that years later, when the churchman had taken the books with him to Alexandria and was killed in one of the frequent riots in the city, Julian asked to have the library saved for his own collection. He knew most of them like the old friends they were during his lonely years at Macellum.

When Julian neared his eighteenth birthday, he received an unexpected visitor, who set his life on a new course. We have no record that the emperor Constantius had ever met Julian face to face before this point, but now on his way to the East the ruler of the Roman world made a detour through Cappadocia to meet his cousins in person. Julian and his brother Gallus must have been terrified at being presented to the man who had murdered their father and could end their lives with a word. But the still childless Constantius was determined to meet these young men who were his closest surviving blood relatives. If he judged them a threat, they would be executed immediately. If not, they could be set on the road to power as future rulers of Rome.

The details of what happened during the visit of Constantius are unknown, but it is safe to say that the emperor was satisfied with the boys and decided to keep them alive for the immediate future. The two cousins were transferred to the court in Constantinople, where Gallus received military and administrative training under close supervision. Julian seems to have shown little promise as a soldier and so, being less of a threat, was allowed to continue his studies under two of the leading scholars of the day, the pagan Nicocles and the Christian Hecebolius. Both were masters of rhetoric, the art of public speaking, reasoning, and presentation that was crucial for any Roman gentleman. But Julian was already so skilled as a scholar and speaker that Constantius soon grew alarmed that the young man would attract a following at court. To counter this, the emperor sent him away from the life of the capital back across the Sea of Marmara to the university town of Nicomedia, not far from his grandmother's estate.

Though near Constantinople, Nicomedia was a world away from the cosmopolitan bustle of the imperial court—and that, of course, was part of the emperor's plan to isolate Julian from anyone who might try to use the bright lad as a focal point of opposition. But by sending Julian to Nicomedia, Constantius inadvertently introduced him to a man who would be one of the most important figures of his life: the renowned pagan scholar Libanius. Born in Syrian Antioch, Libanius was only in his mid-thirties when he was teaching at Nicomedia, but he was already one of the most influential scholars in the Roman Empire. Hecebolius, Julian's tutor in Constantinople, despised Libanius and, having seen his rival expelled from the capital a few years earlier in an academic quarrel, made Julian swear he would not attend any of his lectures while in Nicomedia. Julian was true to his word, and though he probably met Libanius privately, he hired a secretary to record the academic's classes so that he might review them carefully later. Libanius was a celebrated pagan teacher of rhetoric, but many future Christian saints, including John Chrysostom, Basil, and Gregory of Nazianzus, would count him among their most gifted instructors. Although not a Christian, he was wise enough not to antagonize church leaders or the imperial court and was thus able to maintain a leading role in the intellectual life of the empire throughout his long career. He would also become one of the great defenders of Julian when the young man ascended to the throne. But for now in Nicomedia, he became Julian's secret and most influential teacher.

While Julian was still happily a student, Gallus was elevated to the rank of Caesar by Constantius. The earlier emperors Diocletian and Constantine had used the office of Caesar as a kind of emperor-in-training to help with the management of the realm. Although Constantius did not completely trust Gallus, he nevertheless needed a family member to represent him as a visible presence among the citizens in the East since Germanic uprisings were forcing him to spend more of his time in the West. The Persians were also a constant threat to the empire's eastern borders, and the stationing of even an inexperienced Caesar near them might make them think twice before causing trouble on the frontiers.

Julian, meanwhile, was enjoying one of the happiest periods of his life as he made his way around the Aegean meeting and learning from some of the greatest intellectuals of the day. For so many years he had been alone with his books. Now among other students and teachers he was at last able to shine as the brilliant scholar he was. He first traveled south along the coast to the city of Pergamum, where he studied for a time with the elderly Aedesius, a chief proponent of the school of Neoplatonism who had once been a pupil of the famed Iamblichus himself. This philosophy had arisen a century earlier with Plotinus and Porphyry, who reinterpreted the classic teachings of Plato in a metaphysical fashion. Never a precisely defined creed or method, Neoplatonism encompassed many teachings that were to have an enormous influence on thinkers for years to come. Chief among them was the belief found in Plato that a realm of invisible ideas exists that is more real than the visible world around us. In Neoplatonism, the highest of these ideas was the One, a divine force that is the creative and sustaining source of the universe. Neoplatonists did not reject the traditional gods of the Greco-Roman pantheon but saw them instead as representations of the higher universal ideal. And although followers of Neoplatonism held widely differing views on practically every aspect of philosophy, they nonetheless shared a common spiritual outlook which would have seemed uncomfortably mystical to many earlier

Greek intellectuals, perhaps even to Plato himself. The fact that on a broader level Neoplatonism could be an attractive philosophy to Christian thinkers was not lost on those in the church who sought wisdom in Greek philosophy. Many Christians and Jews at the time, as well as Muslims in the centuries to come, were drawn to the same compelling ideas that Julian was encountering in his studies.

It would not have taken much of a change in his life's path for Julian to become a traditional Christian intellectual with a tendency toward Neoplatonic spiritualism. Many such thinkers made up an integral and faithful component of the church at the time. Why Julian chose to reject Christianity outright is one of the puzzles in interpreting his life, but the brutal hypocrisy of having his father and family murdered by a Christian emperor must be among the chief causes. Another may be that Julian was profoundly drawn to magic in a way that Christianity would never allow. A branch of Neoplatonism emphasized direct divine intervention in the world in the form of miracles and supernatural experiences. Many Neoplatonists scoffed at the very idea of such tawdry wonders, but others sought a mystical experience with the One through what some would dismiss as sorcery. For an impressionable and lonely young man like Julian, the hope of experiencing a personal and visible connection to the spiritual forces of the universe must have been powerful indeed.

Among the professors Julian studied with in Pergamum were the two Neoplatonists, Eusebius and Chrysanthius, who had also been pupils of Aedesius. They emphasized a decidedly positive view of the miraculous over the more logical analysis of many of their fellow Neoplatonic scholars. Eusebius spoke admirably yet somewhat grudgingly of the eloquence of another pupil of Aedesius named Maximus of Ephesus, though he warned that Maximus's preference for magic over intellectual reasoning was too much even for his own taste. He claimed that Maximus, who after Julian's death would be executed by a Christian emperor for conspiracy, could cause the torches of the dark goddess Hecate to miraculously burst into flame at his command but warned Julian not to be impressed by such cheap tricks, even if they were a genuine manifestation of divine power. For Julian such tales were all he needed. He immediately left Pergamum and journeyed to Ephesus to find Maximus.

Maximus was thrilled to have a royal pupil and made it his mission to become indispensable to the young prince. It is likely that Maximus, among other secret activities, initiated Julian into the mysteries of Mithras, whose worship was exclusively male, had ties across the empire, and promised eternal life to its members. Although Julian's conversion to paganism may have been years in the making, the future emperor later dated his rejection of Christianity to his time with Maximus. However, Julian was anything but a fool and knew that to publicly reveal his religious conversion would mean imprisonment and execution. Constantius could overlook a young Christian philosopher who dabbled in harmless Neoplatonism, but a professed pagan who openly rejected the church was a potential threat to the family's hold on the empire. And so for the time being, and indeed for the next few years, Julian followed the outward forms of Christian life and worship as expected. With his deep knowledge of holy scripture, liturgy, and theology, he had no difficulty pretending to be a model Christian. Only a small circle of intimates knew the shocking truth that one of the heirs to the imperial throne was in fact a pagan.

The final stop on Julian's studies was the city of Athens, where for a time he attended lectures and mingled happily with other students, including the future Bishop Gregory, who would later write so scathingly about him. Gregory claimed he knew from the moment he met Julian that the young man was a secret pagan, but this is most unlikely. Julian was scrupulous in his imitation of the Christian life and revealed his true beliefs to no one he did not trust completely.

Julian's time at Athens at the center of the Greek intellectual world was one of the high points of his life. Although the city had long since ceased to be of political importance, it was still a famous university town with an ancient and glorious heritage. Julian must have spent many hours visiting the schools founded by Plato and Aristotle, marveling at the Parthenon and other buildings on the Acropolis, and wandering the Agora, where Socrates had first practiced his craft as a philosopher. It was a brief but glorious calm before the storm that would soon envelop him.

Julian's likelihood of someday inheriting the purple robes of the emperor — or possibly meeting his death — increased greatly when his brother Gallus was recalled and executed by Constantius. Gallus had served adequately as Caesar in the East while he was based in Antioch, resisting both a Persian incursion and a Jewish rebellion, but he was by nature a cruel and thoughtless man who had none of Julian's intelligence or prudence. He quarreled constantly with imperial officials and refused to follow directives from the emperor. At last Constantius had had enough of his upstart young cousin and ordered him to report to the court, then in residence in Milan. Even Gallus must have known what was coming next, but there was nowhere he could run. On his way to Italy, Gallus was summarily stripped of his title of Caesar and executed near the city of Pola, in the Balkans.

Julian, who had never been close to his brother, was nonetheless both angered and terrified when he heard the news. Several years later he would write in a letter to the Athenians that although his brother was not fit to rule he did not deserve to die. Gallus was Julian's last link to his childhood, and in spite of the chasm between the two siblings his death must have left Julian feeling completely alone in a very hostile world. And how long could he himself now expect to live? Constantius would have preferred a blood relative as his heir and as an assistant in administering the empire, but he was perfectly capable of killing both his cousins and removing any threat to the throne if he deemed it expedient. At twenty-four, Julian was the only other member of Constantine's family still alive. When the summons came for him to attend the court in Milan, Julian surely said a prayer to the gods. He was told that charges of conspiracy and treason had been lodged against him and that the emperor would decide his fate in person.

Julian later wrote that he had no designs on power and wanted only to be a student, a claim that is in fact likely to have been true at that point. A young man of sincere intellectual devotion, watched over day and night by imperial spies, would be unlikely to have the opportunity to plot a rebellion against the throne. But discovering the truth about Julian was hardly the goal of the court in Milan. The imperial chamberlain, a eunuch named Eusebius, led the faction of those who wanted Julian executed as a potential threat to Constantius and his own power. But Julian did have an advocate in the emperor's wife, Eusebia, who had apparently investigated her husband's cousin with some care and discovered that he was a shy and brilliant young man who could be nurtured and possibly trusted to help ease her husband's heavy load.

The empress Eusebia was to hold a unique position in Julian's life. She was from a noble Greek family of Thessaloniki in Macedonia. Her father had served the empire loyally as a military commander and had been honored with the rank of consul. Young Eusebia was beautiful as well as highly educated and a lover of books.

Early in his rising career she had caught the eye of Constantius, who saw her as an adornment to his rule and a worthy ally in his ongoing struggle for power. As the mother of his future sons, she would, he hoped, play a key role in the continuation of his dynasty. She was from a Christian family, though of the Arian sect favored by many of the noble families.

To Julian, Eusebia would always be his savior and advocate. In his panegyric to the empress written during his time in Gaul, the young Caesar overflows with praise for his patroness, though in a different way from his orations of praise for her husband: "Now the empress no sooner heard the words spoken against me — not reports of wrongdoing but mere suspicions — than she began to carefully investigate them. She would not consider any lies or un-just slander, but was persistent in her inquiry."[5]

Although couched in the typically florid style of panegyrics, Julian's praise of Eusebia has a sincerity normally absent in the genre and certainly lacking in the speeches for her husband. When he compares her to Penelope, the wise and matchless wife of Odys-seus, the reader cannot help but feel that he truly means it. Eusebia becomes to him the ideal woman, equal to no other. For Julian, who never knew his mother and had no sisters or close female friends, it was an understandable though perhaps dangerous tendency to find an older woman in his life who had been kind to him and idealize her beyond a standard any woman could live up to. It also blinded him to whatever harm she might do him in the future.

Constantius was in a difficult position. The Germans had been making ever more frequent raids into Gaul, and usurpers were always threatening his throne. Moreover, he still had no children; his sudden death could throw the empire into turmoil and civil war. Even if only serving as a figurehead, Julian as a member of Con-stantine's family could be useful to Constantius. As Julian made his way to Milan, the factions arguing for and against Julian's execution vied for the ear of the emperor, though Constantius remained silent. But by the time Julian arrived in Milan, his fate had been decided. As Julian firmly believed, it was Eusebia who made the difference, and he was duly grateful to her for the rest of his life.

In November 355, Julian was named to the high office of Caesar by Constantius and ordered to report to his new military headquarters in Gaul. His days as a student were forever over. He was now the second-ranking officer in the empire and the presumptive heir. From now on he would be the chief lieutenant in the service of Constantius, the Christian emperor of Rome. His future was secure — if only he could survive the challenges that lay ahead.

CHAPTER THREE

Gaul

J ulian was, according to the ancient sources, a rather average man in appearance.[1] He was neither short nor tall, handsome nor ugly, but he was surprisingly strong, with broad shoulders, and a good runner. He had a straight nose, bright eyes, and fine hair that always lay flat on his head as if it had just been combed. His one unusual feature was a thick, muscular neck, confirmed by images on contemporary coins, which seems to have been a common trait in the family of Constantine. But the quality of Julian most commented on by those who knew him was not his physical appearance but his irrepressible energy. He seemed never to sleep and would spend nights reading whole books, talking endlessly to companions, or writing letters to friends far away. This energy would serve him well in Gaul as he struggled to fight a war, govern a province, and navigate the treacherous waters of the royal family.

To seal the appointment as his new Caesar and to further bind him to the imperial family, Constantius gave Julian his own sister Helena as his bride. The emperor had done the same for Gallus by granting Julian's brother his elder sister Constantia when he became Caesar several years earlier, but the result had been a disastrous mismatch, as Constantia was much older than her new husband and had a cruel nature that only inflamed the worst tendencies of Gallus. Constantius hoped things would go better for Julian. Although Julian could hardly have been thrilled to marry a cousin he may never have met, he knew enough about political alliances to accept the gift with grace. Love in such relationships was neither expected nor required, only loyalty and a good-faith effort to produce male heirs. This was probably a key reason why Constantius wanted Julian to marry Helena. If he were unable to have a son himself, as looked increasingly likely, the emperor might at least have a nephew to groom for the throne. As for Julian, he would perform his conjugal duties faithfully, though without apparent enthusiasm. Of the many charges his enemies would bring against him in years to come, sexual excess or even a moderate carnal interest in either sex was not among them. Julian seems to have had a genuine ascetic temperament and inclination to celibacy. In an imperial court and a wider world, pagan and Christian, drenched in indulgence and indiscretions of the flesh, Julian stands out as a person of almost monastic dedication to sexual purity.

Julian rarely mentions Helena in his writings, and when he does it is, as he himself admits, without emotion: "I should not have resented it if someone had published for the whole world to read all that I ever wrote to my wife, so temperate was it in every respect."[2]

Helena was a devout Christian with a home in Rome who apparently had little interest in literature or academics. She would dutifully accompany Julian to Gaul, but he paid scant attention to her there. His primary emotion toward Helena seems to have been a detached pity, seeing her as a pawn in the same power game as himself. He wished her no ill but had no interest in developing an attachment to her. He spent his nights with friends and books, not with his wife, who had a separate bedroom in their home. Julian visited her only on rare occasions to fulfil his husbandly duties. He was successful at this at least once during his first year in Gaul; Helena became pregnant. The historian Ammianus alleges, however, that the empress Eusebia bribed the midwife present at the delivery to cut the umbilical cord too short and thus kill the infant.[3] It was claimed the empress was jealous because of her own inability to conceive (though it is as likely that the problem lay with Constantius), but one can well wonder if there might be more to the story. Ammianus also charges that in the following year, during a visit by Helena to Rome with her brother and sister-in-law to celebrate twenty years of rule by Constantius, Eusebia poisoned her with a drug that would cause her to miscarry in the future.

But why would Eusebia have fought so hard to keep Julian alive and promote him to Caesar only to prevent him from having children, especially if she were unable to have them herself? Is it worth crediting such reports? Ammianus was unlikely to have deemed such rumors worthy of inclusion in his history if he believed them baseless. If they are true, the most likely explanation is that Eusebia never gave up hope of bearing a son herself for Constantius and saw any potential child of Helena and Julian as a threat. Reports did, in fact, circulate that Eusebia's death a few years later was the result of her experimentation with questionable fertility treatments.

Julian sometimes seems so unfeeling as a husband that we might wonder if such was his nature with everyone. But he was in truth a man of deep compassion, as seen in one of his letters to an otherwise unknown friend named Himerius that probably dates to his time in Gaul: "I could not read without tears the letter you wrote to me after the death of your wife. I was so touched by your terrible grief."[4] Julian loved his friends and cared deeply for their happiness. He was by nature generous to a fault and would gladly share everything he had with those he cared for. He simply was unable to form close relationships with the opposite sex, including his wife, perhaps because he had known so few women during his younger years.

Helena's time in the world was doomed to be short and tragic. Her mother, Fausta, had been executed by her father, Constantine, supposedly for adultery or treason. Helena suffered at least two miscarriages and died several years later without any mention from Julian. If there was any consolation for her brief life, it was that she was buried in a stunning porphyry sarcophagus inside a beautiful mausoleum in Rome. Constantine had begun construction of the church, but in a delayed token of spousal devotion or perhaps simple guilt, it was completed for his wife by Julian.

After his appointment as Caesar, Julian was quickly dispatched to Gaul to provide a visible imperial presence to the volatile and troubled province. The Romans had annexed Gaul four hundred years earlier during the celebrated conquest of Julius Caesar. For most of that time it had been a relatively peaceful and productive corner of the Roman world. But Gaul had also been a frontier province, with the warlike Germanic tribes constantly threatening to cross the Rhine and invade the Roman lands to the west. By war, threats, and diplomacy, the emperors had for the most part kept the various German tribes on their side of the river for hundreds of years. The legions had even recruited soldiers and officers from among the Germans for the Roman army, teaching them Latin and paying them well. Some traveled back to their homelands at the end of their service as Romanized as any citizens of the empire, and not a few returned as Christians, though most often Arians. Some of the Germans who now threatened Rome in Gaul were as wild as imperial propaganda claimed, but many were "civilized" and talented war leaders who had been well trained in Roman ways.

When the usurper Magnentius had rebelled a few years earlier, Constantius had invited a tribe of Germans to cross the Rhine, so long as they pledged to fight against the rebellious general on his behalf. The plan had worked, but it had also destabilized Gaul and opened the way for more Germans to migrate over the river. It was Julian's assignment to rally the troops as a visible member of the royal family and push the Germans back across the Rhine. Constantius knew that if Gaul fell into permanent chaos, Britain would be lost as well. The Germans would then be on the doorstep of Italy and the entire western half of the empire would face collapse.

Julian's success in Gaul was of the greatest importance to Constantius, though the emperor understandably did not completely trust his cousin. The young man swore his loyalty to the throne, but Constantius knew he had not forgotten the murder of his father and family, including the recent execution of his brother Gallus. If any other member of the imperial family had been available to lead the army in Gaul, Constantius surely would have given the position of Caesar to him. But Julian was quite simply the only one left alive. He had no training in war or administration and no experience leading the hardened men of the legions. He was a twenty-four-year-old student of Greek philosophy who probably knew just enough Latin to address the troops. He had spent his entire life in the East among scholars, eunuchs, and books. Any reasonable person who wagered on the chances of Julian's success in Gaul would have given him very poor odds.

In the years to come, Julian would write that Constantius had always wanted him to fail and never given him the men or authority he needed to succeed as a Caesar. He claimed that he was allowed little more than to wear a uniform and parade a life-size image of Constantius about to show the local populations. Although Constantius personally accompanied him for a short distance as he rode north out of Milan in the winter of 355, Julian argued that the emperor was unsupportive in every other way, including granting him only a few hundred troops to march with him for his army in Gaul—though he failed to mention the tens of thousands of troops already there waiting to serve him. When he reached his province, he grumbled that he was constantly overseen by military men and senior imperial administrative officials. In these charges and complaints, Julian shows himself disingenuous and unjust. No reasonable emperor would have given Julian immediate and absolute authority over the army and government of Gaul. Julian was a young and unproven scholar who had done nothing to prepare for war in Gaul aside from reading Julius Caesar's accounts, written centuries earlier. In truth Constantius had placed tremendous trust in Julian by granting him the rank of Caesar and sending him to Gaul in the first place. Of course the emperor had no other choice if he wanted a member of the royal family present there, but he would show himself willing to grant increased power to Julian as he spent more time in Gaul and proved to be a capable and sometimes brilliant leader. In spite of Julian's self-serving protests in later writings, Constantius was giving him the chance of a lifetime.

Julian had only a few companions with him when he first arrived in Gaul, and fewer people he could trust. Most of those sent to help him govern understandably owed their primary loyalty to Constantius, even if their desire to serve the young Caesar was sincere. Julian felt as if he were being constantly spied on and that everything he did was being reported back to the emperor—because it was. But even officials appointed by Constantius could be helpful if given a chance. One of the best of these was a eunuch named Eutherius, who had been kidnapped from his native land of Armenia as a boy and sold to a Roman merchant as a slave. By hard work and natural talent he eventually bought his way out of servitude and came to work for the imperial administration in Milan. Although Julian did not trust him at first, Eutherius proved a true friend and faithful adviser. He served Julian in Gaul as his court chamberlain, a grand title for what was essentially the chief of staff over Julian's small group of provincial officials. Eutherius earned Julian's respect at the beginning of his time in Gaul by directly reprimanding the young Caesar for un-Roman levity, a lesson Julian would come to appreciate. The eunuch was also a devout pagan from an officially Christian country, a situation Julian could readily appreciate. In time to come Julian would appoint Eutherius as his personal representative to Constantius to defend his actions in Gaul and assure the emperor of his loyalty. As Julian later wrote to Eutherius in a time of trouble, "I am alive and have been saved by the gods, so offer sacrifices to them in thanks on my behalf. And let your offering be not for me alone but for all of us who faithfully follow the ways of the gods. If you have time, please join me in Constantinople. I should be very honored to have you there with me."[5] Eutherius would long outlive Julian and retire to Rome respected by Christians and pagans alike. That he could gain the confidence and trust of men like Constantius and Julian both at the same time is a testimony to a remarkable man.

Another key figure in Julian's life in Gaul was Saturninus Secundus Salutius (sometimes called Sallustius or Sallust), an older man of Gaulish origin who became a mentor to the young Caesar and a guide for him in the ways of both the imperial court and his native land of Gaul. Salutius was a fellow pagan and follower of the Neoplatonic philosophy so admired by Julian. He was a new Mardonius to Julian and held in Julian's mind the same respect as his

childhood tutor. Salutius was also greatly respected by most of the
Christian and pagan factions around Constantius and by the generals and administrators in Gaul. He was a key ally of Julian's and
provided an important and supportive link to the many disparate
and quarreling factions around him. But in time the officials surrounding Constantius grew jealous and worried about the old man's
closeness to Julian and convinced the emperor to recall him from
Gaul. Julian was in no position to object, so he wrote a touching
speech of consolation and farewell to Salutius in which he expressed
his gratitude and friendship: "We two have shared many sorrows
and also joys in both deeds and words, in affairs public and private,
at home and on the battlefield."[6] Julian needed a father figure like
Salutius in his life and dearly missed him when he was recalled.
But Julian would stay in close contact with Salutius even after his
mentor left Gaul and would rely on him greatly after becoming
emperor.

There is no evidence at this point, in spite of the extensive imperial spy network, that Constantius or anyone else at court suspected that Julian was no longer a faithful Christian. The young Caesar was meticulous in his attendance at Christian services and spoke
only with the greatest respect for the church. Although Julian would
gather about him in Gaul a small coterie of pagan philosophers as
his companions, this was only to be expected of someone with his
scholarly interests. Many in the senior leadership of the army were
openly pagans but loyally served the Christian emperor, and Constantius had no objections as long as they performed their military
services well. The population of the empire itself at this time, especially in western provinces such as Gaul, was overwhelmingly
pagan, though there were bishops and thriving congregations in
all the major cities, such as Paris and Lyon. In the countryside of Gaul,
a Christian seeking to attend church would have to have ridden long

and far to worship with others. Open paganism may not have been an option for Julian while Constantius ruled, but Christians outside the imperial family were still a minority.

On the road to Gaul Julian learned that events in his new province had gone from bad to worse. The Franks had just captured the important city of Cologne on the west bank of the Rhine in northeast Gaul. Cologne had been a cornerstone of Roman control in the province since the days of Emperor Augustus more than three centuries earlier. It had long been the headquarters of the Rhine fleet and the site of a large veterans' colony for retired legionnaires. To lose Cologne was to open all Gaul to invasion by the Franks and other German tribes.

But there was little Julian could do about the Germans in the middle of winter. He therefore made his way to the Roman town of Vienne on the Rhône River south of Lyon to take command of his troops and wait for warmer weather. It was here that Julian received word from court that he had been appointed consul along with Constantius for the coming year. The two consuls of Rome had traditionally held chief executive power over the Roman domains since the earliest days of the republic more than eight hundred years earlier, but since the rise of the empire the office had been merely a symbolic, though important, honor given by the emperor. If nothing else, years were still marked by the names of the two annual consuls. For Constantius to share the role with Julian was a small but significant vote of confidence in his young Caesar.

In response Julian composed a panegyric to Constantius which still survives. A panegyric was a highly formal, conventional, and often cloying piece of praise literature that was not necessarily sincere. Julian's hymn to Constantius is an obvious attempt to win the emperor's favor and prove his loyalty by singing with Homeric glory the praises of his ruler's wartime valor and imperial talents: "I have long desired, my most mighty emperor, to sing the praises of your bravery and accomplishments, to tell of your glorious battles, and how you overcame tyrants."[7] Julian follows the standard formula in such praise literature, highlighting the noble ancestors of Constantius, particularly his father, Constantine: "His military genius was obvious from his achievements and needs no words from me. He strode across the whole world suppressing tyrants, but never those who ruled justly. He inspired his subjects with such affection that his veterans still remember his generosity and to this day honor him as if he were a god."[8] Of course it did no harm to remind Constantius that Constantine was Julian's own grandfather. The ties of blood the two shared might just keep him alive.

But the majority of the panegyric focuses on Constantius himself: "Your father's achievements were many and brilliant. Some of these I have mentioned but others I must omit for the sake of brevity. Still, the most notable achievement of Constantine — if I may be bold enough to say and hope that you agree — was that he begat, raised, and trained you."[9] Julian goes on throughout the rest of the piece to praise everything from Constantius's superb speaking style to his skill as a gifted administrator and especially his success as a defender of Rome against Persians, Gauls, and other enemies of the empire. In keeping with a common trope of classical rhetoric, Julian repeatedly says he has no need to praise the matchless character of Constantius, then goes on to do exactly that at tiresome length.

What is surprisingly missing in this first panegyric is any celebration of Constantius as a defender of the Christian church. It may be that the tradition of these formulaic writings allowed no place for such matters, but the absence could also be Julian avoiding a sensitive subject for Constantius. The emperor was surrounded by Christian factions who were bitterly fighting with one another, much to his dismay and inability to control. The orthodox Christians favored by Constantine had been supplanted at the court of Constantius by moderate Arians so favored by the emperor that he was considered by some to be almost an Arian himself. But in truth Constantius seems to have cared much more for maintaining his power than for following a particular teaching of Christianity. He mostly wanted leaders of the church to keep their peace and stop causing him trouble. Julian was therefore much safer focusing on conventional praise of Constantius as a king and general in the mode of Alexander the Great, the sixth-century BCE Persian emperor Cyrus the Great, and Caesar Augustus.

But in spite of the severe limitations of the genre, this panegyric to the emperor does give us our first extended evidence of Julian as a superb writer and literary stylist. Julian also tellingly makes a point in the work of absolving Constantius of the executions of his family members after the death of Constantine. Julian was clearly trying to convince the emperor that he harbored no ill will toward the man who had murdered his father. We know from Julian's later writings that this was untrue, and it is doubtful he fooled Constantius, but the soothing words had at least been said. Whether during this cold first winter in Gaul Julian was already dreaming of overthrowing Constantius is doubtful. It is more likely that the new Caesar was simply glad to be alive and hoping to get through the coming year without ending up dead on a battlefield.

As the fighting season began in the summer of 356, Julian received disturbing reports that the strategic town of Autun, north of Vienne, was under siege. Roving bands of Germans were raiding farms and villages throughout central Gaul, taking advantage of the vacuum created by the lack of Roman leadership in the province. Julian quickly assembled his army and rushed to Autun, where he drove away the invaders and marked his first military victory. His previous experience with fighting had been confined to the pages of books, but on the field at last he found that he had an unexpected talent and enthusiasm for warfare. He decided to press farther north to relieve other communities that were under German threat. Near modern Troyes he came across an advance band of raiders from the particularly fierce and troublesome Germanic Alamanni confederation and defeated them handily. The Alamanni had often cooperated with Rome to contain other Germans on the east side of the Rhine, but like other tribes they were now taking advantage of unrest in Gaul. They would become Julian's most unyielding adversaries during his years there.

An intriguing story survives that at about this time a young Italian cavalry officer named Martin serving in the army of Julian came before his commander and refused to accept a bonus payment that was being distributed to the soldiers. Martin said he was quitting the legions soon and did not feel right about accepting money since he would not be fighting the Germans: "Until now, Caesar, I have served you in battle, but the time has come for me to serve God. Let someone who intends to fight have the bonus. I am now a soldier of Christ and will kill no more, as it is against the will of God."[10] Julian reportedly grew furious at such insubordination and declared that the young soldier was simply a coward trying to save his own skin. But Martin declared he would gladly stand alone between the two armies in the next battle armed with nothing but a cross if his general doubted the sincerity of his faith. Julian decided to call his bluff and make him do just that, but the next day a message of surrender came from the nearby Germans, thus sparing Martin death as a martyr for Christ. Whether there is any truth to this tale is debatable, set as it is in Christian hagiography, but if true it would have been a fascinating meeting between two young men who would one day rise to great fame in very different ways — Julian as the last pagan emperor of the Roman Empire and the future Saint Martin of Tours, one of the greatest holy men in Christian history.

Far from hindering Julian, Constantius seems to have encouraged his Caesar to assert himself and provided him with the men and resources he needed to help bring Gaul under control that summer. In later works Julian liked to portray himself as the sole savior of the Gaulish lands during his first year in command, but in fact Constantius was nearby in Switzerland most of the time with another Roman army and was almost certainly working in coordination with Julian to put pressure on the German forces. Keeping Constantius regularly apprised of his actions, Julian pressed north to Reims, moving himself between the Germans and Paris. There he joined forces with the experienced Roman commander Marcellus, who was none too pleased to have a young scholar ordering his army about. From Reims, Julian boldly moved east to Metz on the Moselle River to be closer to the German war bands that had crossed the Rhine and seized towns along the west bank of the river in Roman territory. Julian was not at all intimidated by his enemy and advanced eastward, relieving towns along the way, until he came at last to the Rhine itself. To inspire his men to fight even harder than they already were doing, he offered a bounty of gold for the head of any German warrior they killed in battle — a gruesome gesture that would have shocked his fellow philosophy students in Athens. He finally recaptured the Roman city of Cologne in September, just as the campaign season in northern Gaul was coming to an end. After installing a garrison of Roman troops and securing the town, Julian established his winter headquarters at Sens to the south of Paris. He must have been tempted to return to the warmth of southern

Gaul before the snows swept the countryside, but he prudently chose to remain in the north. Julian's unhappy general Marcellus was given most of the troops and established a winter camp near Sens, while Julian set up his military and administrative command within the walled city.

It had been an astonishingly successful few months of fighting for the new Caesar and a pleasing surprise to almost everyone at court, including Constantius, who congratulated Julian warmly and appointed him consul again for the following year. But no one was happier than Julian himself, who had surely harbored many doubts when he first marched into Gaul as to whether he would be able to command an army successfully. Many Gaulish towns were still under foreign control, large bands of German warriors continued to roam the countryside, and plenty of invading tribes were threatening to cross the Rhine when spring returned, but the summer of 356 was a stunning success for Julian in his new role as general of the legions.

Julian was looking forward to a peaceful winter at his headquarters to reorganize the government of Gaul and prepare for the next campaign season, but the Germans chose not to cooperate. Unexpectedly for the season, a large band of Germans descended on Sens and besieged the city while Julian was trapped inside. The Roman general Marcellus was nearby with thousands of troops, but he deliberately chose not to come to his Caesar's aid. We might wonder whether Marcellus had colluded with the German warriors attacking Sens to kill or capture Julian and thus return control of the Roman army in Gaul to himself. Regardless, even without the help of Marcellus and his men, Julian rallied his small band of soldiers and struck back against the besieging Germans, driving them from the town. Constantius was furious with Marcellus when he received word that the general had abandoned Julian. In a strong show of support, Constantius dismissed Marcellus from the army and sent him back in disgrace to his hometown in the Balkans. Marcellus, in a final attempt to save his command, dispatched riders to Constantius accusing Julian of being a headstrong commander and a potential threat to the power of the emperor. Julian quickly learned of the charges and sent his own representatives to Constantius to argue for his competency and loyalty. Tellingly, Constantius sided with Julian against his own general. It was a clear show of affirmation for his Caesar against the entrenched military establishment of the legions and an even clearer signal that Constantius had trust in Julian. That trust was undoubtably tempered by a reasonable caution about what his cousin would do in the future, but for the time being Constantius was giving Julian his support.

The summer of 357 began with Julian preparing for what would be his greatest year as a military leader in Gaul, in spite of the setbacks he would soon face. He left his headquarters at Sens and marched his army to lands just west of the Rhine near the city of Strasbourg. He was working with a new infantry commander named Barbatio, who had once been the commander of the household troops of his brother Gallus—and had then arrested Gallus for execution at the orders of Constantius. Barbatio was an ambitious and treacherous figure whom Julian had no good reason to trust. Nevertheless, Julian ordered him to advance with twenty-five thousand foot soldiers to catch the rebellious Alamanni between their two armies and crush them. These Germans had already been on the move that summer and were raiding as far south as Lyon from their base in Gaulish lands to west of the Rhine. Julian knew they would soon return north, so it was an ideal opportunity to trap the Alamanni between two Roman armies. Julian had even built a bridge of boats across the Rhine to pursue any survivors who might try to flee back into Germany.

But whether through treachery or sheer incompetence, Barbatio allowed the Alamanni to destroy the bridge Julian had built and return to their base unhindered. The Germans then overran Barbatio's army, though the general himself escaped. Julian later claimed that Barbatio had been working with Constantius to allow the Germans to defeat him, but this seems unlikely unless Constantius were willing to risk all of Gaul just to hinder his cousin. In response to the Alamanni raids, Julian ordered his men to destroy their farms west of the Rhine. Constantius had granted them this land several years earlier in return for serving Rome, though they had done a bad job of it, turning instead to raiding Roman lands. Still, the Alamanni had the audacity to send envoys to Julian claiming he had broken the agreement they had with the emperor. Julian was so incensed he broke one of the fundamental rules of ancient diplomacy and had the envoys put in chains as spies.

The Alamanni were furious and gathered more than thirty thousand warriors to destroy Julian's army and drive the Romans out of eastern Gaul once and for all. Julian had fewer than half that number of troops under his command, but remembering that Julius Caesar had faced similar odds many times and prevailed, he decided to take an enormous risk and meet the Germans on the battlefield near Strasbourg on the Rhine.

Julian's own account of the battle is lost, but Ammianus, Libanius, and others help piece together the events that followed. The Romans arrived near the Rhine on a hot day after a long march of several hours. Julian and his men could see the Germans gathering on a low hill by the river with a thick forest to one side. The legions were tired, but they were professional soldiers and were ready to follow their commander into battle. Their training and discipline were the only advantages they had in what they knew would be a fight for their lives. The Germans, however, were brimming with confidence, having the advantage of higher terrain and numbers far greater than the legions. Nonetheless, they were non-Roman warriors who believed in the glory of individual combat rather than adherence to group tactics. They were also a mixed lot of veteran warriors and recent recruits, some with no experience in facing the skilled and highly organized soldiers of the Roman legions. Even so, the Alamanni king, Chnodomar, a giant of a man who was no fool and no stranger to Roman battle tactics, was confident of an easy victory. He had beaten the legions before and had spies on the other side informing him of every detail of the Roman army's movements and struggles.

Julian gathered his men about him after their long march to speak to them. Although better known as a quiet scholar, he was also a skilled orator and fine actor with a great sense of dramatic timing. He began by stating that the army was tired after its journey and should put away any thought of fighting the Germans that day since they were not rested enough to face their formidable opponent. Then, as Julian had arranged, one of his lieutenants shouted out asking the troops if they wanted to let the Germans run away in the night when the legions could beat them here and now. A roar grew up among the soldiers demanding that they face and destroy the enemy right away, and they began to pound their spears against their shields in the time-honored sign that they were ready for a fight. Julian then acceded to their wishes, as he had planned all along, and prepared the men for battle.

Julian lined up his veteran troops in a classic formation, with his lieutenant Severus commanding the cavalry on the left of his line, the infantry positioned in the center with himself as leader, and more armored horsemen to the right. Chnodomar matched them across the field with his enormous infantry in the center and he himself facing Julian's right, ready to tear through the Roman lines and outflank the legions. Chnodomar's nephew Serapion was meanwhile hiding in the trees facing Julian's left with two thousand men ready to pour forth at the right moment, a classic trick of Julius Caesar's that the Germans had learned.

The fight that followed, known as the Battle of Strasbourg, was one of the largest conflicts Gaul had seen for centuries. It began when Julian's commander Severus went forward with his men and engaged Serapion's eager soldiers, who had emerged from hiding too soon. The Roman horse were able to counter these German foot soldiers and keep them from flanking the legions. Julian, meanwhile, rode forward with his men until he was within range of the enemy archers. He then gave the order for his whole army to advance. Chnodomar followed suit and led his men on foot into the fray, attacking the left wing of the Roman line. After a fierce clash, Severus and his cavalry managed to push them back. Julian, moving to the Roman right, was having a harder time. The Germans pounded the legions and gradually forced them to retreat, but Julian refused to give in and rallied his men from the front lines.

The mass of the German army, meanwhile, was hitting the Roman center hard and gaining ground as the legions slowly fell back. Not until the reserve of Roman auxiliaries, many of them German in origin, came up from behind and joined the fight in the center did the Romans began to gain the upper hand. Still, the Alemanni were not ready to give up and pushed furiously one last time against the weary Roman lines until the legions broke. Now the battle became a contest of who wanted to survive the most, with Romans and Germans hacking at each other at close quarters without mercy. But it was the Alemanni who finally broke and turned to run.

Julian rallied his exhausted troops and chased the retreating Alamanni into the swamps on the banks of the Rhine, where they panicked. Many tried to swim across the river or flee to islands in the river, thinking the Romans would not pursue them, but Julian did not intend to let them go so easily. At the end of the day the Rhine ran red with German blood. At least six thousand Alamanni had died, and their king, Chnodomar, had been captured when his horse slipped in the bloody mud. The Romans, remarkably, lost no more than three hundred soldiers, a testament to their discipline in the face of horrendous fighting and to Julian's leadership. Following Roman tradition, the victorious Caesar sent King Chnodomar as a prisoner to Constantius in Milan, who subsequently celebrated a triumph over the Germans in his own name. It was customary for an emperor to claim credit for any victory by his commanders, but it angered Julian that his cousin enjoyed the fruits of a hard-fought battle he had played no part in winning.

After the fighting was done, Julian crossed the Rhine to destroy the villages and farms of the Alamanni who lived on the far side. This was meant as a clear warning to the Germans that the river would not protect them in the future, should they attack Roman territory. Julian then marched north to face the Franks, who had again invaded the area around Cologne. He and Severus pushed them back and surrounded their protected forts, where Julian starved them into surrender after two months. Julian admired the warrior spirit of the pagan Franks and sent the survivors to Constantius for service as auxiliaries in the Roman army, though far from Gaul. The fact that he did not keep them for his own army is an acknowledgment that their service so close to home risked rebellion, but it is also a testimony to his continued loyalty to Constantius. If Julian had been plotting a revolt after Strasbourg, he surely would not have added to the emperor's forces.

And so as 357 drew to a close, Julian completed his second year as Caesar in Gaul by withdrawing to winter quarters in the city of Paris. He had entered his province as a young student of Greek philosophy with no experience in war or leadership. Now, at the age of twenty-six, he was a proven commander who had shown great daring and ability in leading some of the toughest men on earth into battle. Like all great military leaders, he had shown that he was unafraid to join his men on the front lines to risk death alongside them. For this they loved and embraced him as their own. Inspiring such loyalty from the men under him was an essential quality for a successful Roman general. It was also a dangerous challenge to a standing emperor if that loyalty were given to a man of royal blood who might have designs on the throne. Although Constantius was pleased that Julian had greatly reduced the immediate German threat to Gaul, he was aware that he had created a prince and potential rival who might rise up against him. For now though, the emperor needed Julian to stay in Gaul. Whether he could trust Julian in the long term remained to be seen.

Julian spent most of the year after the Battle of Strasbourg in the northern reaches of Gaul near the mouth of the Rhine. The Roman hold on this swampy land had been tenuous for years, and recently a group of uninvited Franks had settled there, disrupting the grain trade between Gaul and Britain. While the Franks were negotiating with his representatives for permission to reside where they had already established their farms, Julian attacked and destroyed them. He then established new Roman forts in the Rhine delta and increased the number of ships in the grain fleet sailing between Britain and Gaul. He spent the rest of the summer on the other side of the Rhine subduing tribes and accepting the submission of German chiefs. He then retired again to Paris to busy himself with administrative work in Gaul during the winter. With him was his friend the young physician and fellow pagan Oribasius. After his work for the day was done, Julian would spend the cold dark nights writing letters to friends in the East, including Libanius in Antioch and the Neoplatonic philosophers Priscus and Maximus. He knew that Maximus was unlikely to make the long journey west to visit him, but he tried several times to persuade Priscus to come: "After your last letter I sent Archelaus to you with my own correspondence and gave him the requested travel documents for you. If you'll dare to sail the sea with the help of the gods, I'll provide you with everything you might need for the journey—unless it's just that you dread the boorish ways of the Gauls and the freezing weather here."[11]

But it was the Greek doctor Oribasius who was the most constant companion of Julian for the rest of his life. Oribasius was about a decade older than Julian and had received his medical education in Alexandria. They had met at Pergamum, the hometown of Oribasius, a few years earlier, while Julian was still a student. In a world in which many physicians struggled to earn a living, the appointment as chief medical officer to a rising Caesar was a coup, but the relationship between the two men was close and sincere. Julian made few friends in his lifetime, so he was pleased to have Oribasius near to him through all the trials he came to face. Medical scholars would long remember Oribasius for his surviving encyclopedic work, the *Compilations*, based on the studies of Galen, the most famous doctor of the ancient world. But Julian would rely on Oribasius for more than medical care. A story survives that he once sent his friend to the oracle of Apollo at Delphi to see if there were anything a pagan emperor could do to promote the ancient shrine. Oribasius reportedly returned with a sad message from the priests:

Tell the king that the glorious hall has fallen.
Phoebus Apollo has no dwelling here,
no laurel branch, no prophetic spring.
The sacred waters that once spoke are silent.[12]

The verse comes from a later Byzantine source and may be pure Christian invention, but it echoes a feeling that was surely in the air in Julian's day: the old ways of the gods were passing away—unless someone could preserve them.

By the end of the year in Gaul, Julian had largely finished the task assigned to him by the emperor of restoring order and prosperity to the Roman province. He had proven himself more than competent as a military commander and provincial administrator. He had, in short, far exceeded all the expectations of Constantius and the imperial court. To affirm his loyalty to the crown, Julian composed another panegyric to the glory of the emperor. It was as formulaic in its praise of Constantius as the first, but it shows the beginning of a change in Julian. As was common in the genre, he devotes a great deal of the work to a discussion of Plato's vision of the ideal ruler, but then notably neglects to state that Constantius was such a leader. In his lauding of the emperor, Julian also compares the relationship he had with Constantius to that of the young warrior Achilles and the Greek ruler Agamemnon in the *Iliad*: "Kings ought never to behave foolishly, nor use their power without self-control, nor be carried away in their anger like a wild beast that runs away for lack of a bit and rider."[13] Constantius may not have been the scholar Julian was, but he knew his Homer well enough to realize that his Caesar was now portraying himself as the rising star and a superior soldier to the emperor. It was a dangerous and arrogant move for a young general, no matter how great his success in battle. Constantius and his advisers could hardly have failed to notice the new challenge implicit in Julian's poem of praise.

CHAPTER FOUR

Rebellion

In the winter of 359, while Julian was safe at his headquarters in Paris, things were going poorly for the Roman Empire on its eastern borders. The Persians were causing trouble once again. Ever since the days of the Great Kings Darius and Xerxes in the sixth and fifth centuries BCE, the Persians had been a recurring threat to first the Greeks and then the Romans. Unlike the Germans, they were a united empire under a single strong ruler with a large and well-organized professional army. In the previous century they had often bested the Romans and killed or captured emperors but had finally been pushed back to their frontier. Now with the Persian threat once again rising, Constantius had no choice but to turn his attention to the beleaguered Roman lands of Syria and northern Mesopotamia. This meant that he needed troops for his army, and with the Germans quiet for the moment, the emperor decided those troops would come from Julian's forces in Gaul.

On the face of it this was a reasonable decision. Roman soldiers were very expensive to recruit and maintain, as well as being sworn to protect and defend the empire wherever they were needed. But it seemed too convenient to Julian and his supporters then and since that Constantius would choose this moment to severely reduce the number of troops Julian had under his command in Gaul. When the messenger from Constantius arrived at Julian's headquarters in Paris late that winter, he announced that it was the emperor's pleasure that almost half of Julian's army be transferred to service against Persia and that they would leave Gaul immediately. This was particularly awkward for Julian since he had promised his army units from Gaul that they would never have to leave the land where most of them had been born and raised and where their families lived. True, some had recently been temporarily deployed across the channel to fight against the Picts and Scots who were raiding the Roman frontiers of Britain, but Britain was practically next door, and they were there only a brief time. The Persian frontier was more than two thousand miles from Paris, across mountains and seas. The local Gaulish troops were furious at the order and adamant that they would not obey the command of an emperor they did not know, who had not risked his life in battle beside them as their Caesar had.

According to Julian's own words, he had never intended to rebel against Constantius and was taken completely by surprise when his Gaulish troops refused to go to Persia. We know that he indeed summoned to Paris the troops Constantius had demanded, purportedly to send them on their way to service under the emperor. When the troops had assembled in the city, he invited their officers to dine with him one evening. But that same night an anonymous letter criticizing Constantius and his orders was making the rounds through the camp which was so inflammatory that the supporters of the emperor in the city urged Julian to send the troops east immediately to allow the enemies of Constantius no time to stir up trouble. Before Julian could react, however, a large group of soldiers surrounded the headquarters where he and the officers were dining to demand that Julian keep them in Gaul. Then the troops took the ominous step — again, Julian says, without his consent — of declaring him Augustus, a title equal in rank with Constantius's.

Proclamation by the army had long been a road to the imperial purple for rising Roman generals, but it was also the common first step to rebellion and civil war. Julian later wrote that he was taken totally by surprise when the soldiers granted him this honor, but more than a few of his enemies and even some of his friends found his denials hard to believe. By this time Julian was a proven commander in war and an able provincial administrator who missed little of what was going on around him. He was also a keen student of Roman history and knew how to read a crowd. It is very easy to believe — and is in fact likely — that Julian had stage-managed the whole affair in Paris to serve his own ambitions. While it is unlikely he wanted an all-out civil war with Constantius at that moment, it is probable that he was ready to take what he believed was his rightful title of Augustus. He was, after all, a member of the royal family who had saved the western Roman Empire from destruction by the Germans. He knew that if he sent Constantius half his troops, he would not only betray the trust the Gauls had in him but very likely see those same troops marching back behind the banner of Constantius to crush him when the war with Persia was done. Events may have moved faster than Julian had planned, but he knew that unless he acted immediately to claim an equal share as Augustus with Constantius, he would lose his chance forever.

Yet Julian's decision was more than a grab for political power. He honestly believed he had a divine mandate to restore the true religion of the gods in the face of the growing Christian threat. He had seen the hypocrisy of his murderous cousin and the greedy bishops gathered around him. He had also seen how the empire had suffered from foreign invasions and instability under the Christian rule of Constantius. Julian knew that time was running out not just for himself but for the worship of the gods of Rome – Jupiter, Apollo, Minerva, Mars – who had made the empire great. If Christianity were allowed to continue unchecked with its impious denial of those gods, heaven would surely withdraw its blessings from Rome and allow the world to be overcome by darkness. Julian might not be ready to reveal his paganism openly while Constantius still ruled as senior Augustus, but he was determined to provide at the least a counterweight to the Christian court and a voice to the majority of people in the empire who still believed and trusted in the old gods.

Julian was careful to send soothing letters to Constantius de-claring his loyalty to the emperor and claiming he had had no part in his field promotion to the rank of Augustus. He was meticulous in signing all his correspondence as Caesar rather than using his new title. But Constantius, veteran of intrigue and rebellion that he was, believed none of it. The emperor received the news of the events in Paris while he was at Caesarea in Cappadocia, ironically the same place he had imprisoned the younger Julian for six years. Constantius was furious about what he saw as an act of open re-bellion at a time when Rome and the imperial family most needed to unite against the Persian threat. He wrote back to Julian that he was not at all pleased and that he recognized Julian's rank only as Caesar, regardless of what the soldiers in Paris might declare. The emperor then began to make his plans. He would have to confront Persia first since it was the most immediate threat to the empire, but when that enemy was beaten he would turn his attention to his upstart cousin and march west to destroy Julian.

Julian for his part spent the months after the acclamation at Paris strengthening his position and preparing his men for the civil war he was now certain was coming. Julian was a proven general and commander, but he was not foolish enough to underestimate

Constantius. The emperor had a much larger and more experienced army. He was also a cunning and ruthless man when faced with threats against his power, especially from family members. Julian had no doubt that Constantius would attack him as soon as he could. The best Julian could do in the meantime was attempt to gain an advantage against the emperor. He also needed to prepare the people of the empire for what lay ahead and win them over to his side. He began in some cities to mint coins that showed himself and Constantius as joint emperors, while in other towns he portrayed himself alone as Augustus. Since the common people had little contact with rulers aside from the coins they used to buy their bread, it was a clear and powerful message to the citizens of the empire that Julian considered himself at the very least the equal of Constantius.

Whatever his plans against Constantius, Julian was still a faithful defender of the Roman Empire in the West. While he was making plans to move against his cousin, he also waged a lengthy campaign against hostile Germans, crossing the Rhine again and making war against the Franks. This served to subdue the foreigners and prepare Gaul for his coming absence when he marched east to face Constantius, but it also hardened his men for what would surely be a difficult war ahead. Julian was betting that even though his Gaulish soldiers had refused to join the army of the emperor against the Persians, they would be willing to follow him personally away from their home, lured with promises of gold and glory.

After a summer of subduing the Germans, Julian returned to Vienne, where he had spent his first winter in Gaul. Like the good Christian he still pretended to be, he openly celebrated the Feast of Epiphany with the local bishop. That winter in Vienne he also celebrated five years of service as a Caesar, though he conspicuously behaved like an Augustus, wearing a jeweled crown and purple im-

Julian

perial robes. Constantius signaled his own intentions that winter by pointedly not selecting Julian as a consul for the coming year. Instead he chose his ally Florentius along with one of his own staunch supporters, Taurus, who was serving as prefect of Italy. With Taurus in Italy and Florentius now appointed to the province of Il-lyricum in the western Balkans, Constantius planned to block any plans Julian might have of moving south or east toward Constantinople. If his cousin could be isolated in Gaul until the fighting in Persia was finished, it would be much easier to contain the budding rebellion and squelch any hopes Julian might harbor of stirring a popular uprising against the emperor in the East.

But Constantius was doing more than just blocking Julian's movement to the capital. Early in his reign the emperor had conspired with German tribes to wage war on the usurper Magnentius in Gaul, even though this had plunged the Roman province into chaos for years afterward. Now Julian discovered letters, which seem genuine, proving that Constantius was recruiting Vadomar, another king of the Germanic Alamanni, to cross the Rhine from the Black Forest to attack Julian's army in Gaul and devastate the farms and cities of the Roman province. That the emperor was willing to risk all the hard work Julian had put in, as well as the lives of Roman soldiers, to gain a political advantage over his cousin was a shock to even the most loyal of Constantius's supporters in Gaul. But the fact that the he had done the same thing previously to put down a rebellion made the treacherous action all the more credible to the threatened citizens of Gaul. Julian published the letters and had them distributed as far and as widely as he could, even reading them out loud himself to crowds wherever he traveled.

Julian sent soldiers into Germany and captured Vadomar before the king could hide himself away in his dark forests. Under questioning back in Gaul, the German leader confirmed the conspiracy instigated by Constantius. The soldiers and officers of Julian were so furious that they seized the leading supporters of Constantius in the province and were about to kill them when Julian intervened to spare their lives. As treacherous as they were to his cause, he did not want the imperial court or the citizens of the empire to see him as a bloody tyrant. Instead he threw the captives into prison and began to make plans in earnest for a war against the emperor.

By the summer of 361, Julian was ready. He decided to divide his forces into three smaller armies rather than have a single force march across the Balkans toward Constantinople. This was a smart move, as it made his soldiers appear more numerous than their true numbers and inspired confidence in his cause from the Romans in the lands he crossed. Speed was also a hallmark of Julian's enterprises, something he had learned from his studies of the campaigns of Alexander the Great as well as from his own now considerable experience at war. In command of his first army he ordered one of his cavalry officers, Jovian, to ride to Illyricum by way of northern Italy. Another cavalry commander, Nevitta, a low-born man who had worked his way up through the ranks, was sent at speed through the Alps between Italy and the Danube. Julian himself took a mere three thousand men through the Black Forest to the upper reaches of the Danube to a spot where the river became navigable. There he built a fleet and began sailing down the Danube with his forces.

The movement of Julian's three armies east was surprisingly successful, at least at first. When Constantius's prefects Taurus in Italy and Florentius in Illyricum heard of the approaching forces of Jovinus and Nevitta, they promptly panicked and fled their provinces. Julian, meanwhile, was moving down the Danube with his men at a furious pace. By early autumn he was approaching Sirmium, one of the most important cities on the northern frontier and the recent headquarters of Constantius before he had left for

Persia. The loyal commander the emperor had left in his place there could not manage to organize an effective defense of the town, and soon Julian was marching through the streets to strewn flowers and the cheers of the citizens. He was welcomed to the palace of Constantius and treated in every way by the courtiers present as the Augustus he claimed to be. Sirmium was the strategic key to Illyricum, lying as it did at the entrance to the province and controlling all movement up and down the Danube. It was also on the dividing line between the eastern and western regions of the empire. From this point forward, Julian would be moving into the wealthiest, most populous, and most Christian provinces of Rome.

Julian was determined to win the favor of his fellow Romans by entertainments and mercy. He celebrated lavish games at a festival for all the people of Sirmium to attend. He also pardoned the two legions of Constantius he had captured in the city, sending them to Gaul, where he hoped they would prove loyal to him. This was a mistake. They rebelled on their march west and settled into the port city of Aquileia at the head of the Adriatic, where Constantius still had many supporters. Julian fumed at the betrayal of his clemency and ordered both Jovian and Nevitta to divert south on their march to capture Aquileia and neutralize the rebellious legions. In the meantime Julian moved farther down the Danube to the town of Nish, where his uncle Constantine had been born. Nish lay just to the west of the Succi Pass, the gateway to the eastern Balkans and the approach to Constantinople. There he waited for the armies of Jovian and Nevitta to catch up with him so that his forces would be at full strength for the most difficult part of the campaign ahead.

Julian spent the two months he was at Nish writing letters to the towns and cities of the Roman Empire, trying to persuade their citizens of the justice of his claim to the throne and the strength of his case against Constantius. This was an odd move on Julian's part, especially as many of the cities, such as Athens and Sparta, no longer held any real importance in the political world of the fourth century. But the historic and symbolic standing of these towns in Julian's mind overruled such objections. Only his letter to the Athenians survives. In it he praises Athens for the glorious deeds of its forefathers and the devotion of its people to freedom against the forces of tyranny. He portrays himself as grievously wronged by his cousin and drops any pretense of civility toward the emperor who murdered his family: "Six of my cousins—his cousins too!—he killed without mercy, along with my father, who was his own uncle, and another uncle of us both on my father's side, then later my elder brother. He had them all put to death not even bothering with a trial."[1]

There was no going back for Julian now. He had declared in writing his opposition to the emperor and was in open rebellion, leading an army against the ruler of the Roman world. It was an audacious gamble, but he felt he had no choice if he wished to ensure his political survival. He also firmly and sincerely believed the gods were on his side. As cynical as some of his contemporaries and historians of the future might be, Julian genuinely believed he was blessed by the gods of Rome and ordained to overthrow the Christian emperor and his church for the sake of the empire—if only he could survive the war ahead.

History is more often than not driven by vast and powerful economic and social currents beyond the control of any single person and not susceptible to twists of fate. With the perspective of time we can say that the defeat of Julian at the hands of his more powerful and experienced cousin was almost a foregone conclusion, along with the ultimate futility of any attempt to restore the worship of the old gods of Rome. Julian's rebellion should have ended as a historical footnote, with his small army defeated and his head on a spike as a warning from Constantius to other potential traitors. The church should have continued its march to domination in the ancient world undeterred by any organized opposition led by an emperor. All of this is what should have happened—but then history took a most unexpected turn.

Constantius had left the Persian frontier to confront Julian with his massive army and crush him before he could reach the walls of Constantinople. The emperor was in his prime at forty-four years old, full of health and vigor and ready to face and overcome the most recent of many challenges to his reign.

But suddenly in early November at the town of Mopsucrene in Cilicia, Constantius died.

Later, dubious reports say he lived long enough to dictate a letter granting the throne to Julian, but in truth it was a quick and unexpected end to a man who was the consummate survivor in a world of deadly political intrigue. If Constantius had time to give thought to Julian before he breathed his last, those thoughts were surely not kind. But in the end it scarcely mattered, because now a young general and philosopher, the only remaining member of the imperial family, and a secret pagan who was about to reveal himself to the world, was the sole ruler of the entire Roman Empire.

CHAPTER FIVE

Constantinople

Julian was still in the city of Nish preparing for war on the cold winter's day when the messengers from the royal court raced into the palace and dropped to their knees, bearing the news of the death of Emperor Constantius. This was the last thing Julian had expected, and his joy at inheriting the throne so suddenly must have been tempered by the awesome imperial weight which now settled onto his shoulders.

With the death of Constantius, Julian felt the time was at last right to openly declare his paganism. He began by publicly holding animal sacrifices to the gods at Nish, with many soldiers from the army joining him at the altars. The ritual sacrifice of sheep, goats, oxen, and other animals had been fundamental to the act of worshipping the gods in the ancient world since the beginning of civilization. The beasts were led forward, prayers to the gods were recited, then the throats of the animals were cut and warm blood ran in streams from the altar. Less desirable cuts of meat were then placed in the fire so that their sweet smell might rise to the heavens. The better cuts were roasted and eaten by the worshippers in a feast or sold to townspeople in the marketplaces. To Christians such an act was anathema, and devout members of the church would take great care to make sure that none of the meat they dined on at home had been offered to the gods. Although Julian writes of the majority of the army joining him in sacrifice, he does not report the reaction of the sizable number of Christian soldiers among his troops. The sacrifice was a calculated risk on the part of the new emperor, who was betting that the benefits of public sacrifice would improve his standing among the largely pagan army — for keeping the goodwill and support of the army was essential at the start of his reign.

Julian also signaled his paganism by growing a beard. In themselves beards were not opposed by the church, and many priests and bishops went unshaven, but beards were most clearly associated with the philosophers of old, who traditionally wore them. The pagan emperor and Stoic philosopher Marcus Aurelius, a particular hero of Julian's, was perhaps the best known of the emperors to wear a beard, and Julian now clearly identified himself with his celebrated predecessor. The new emperor even struck coins at Nish showing him bearded so that this declaration of his paganism might be seen throughout the empire.

But more than military or political calculations, Julian's open show of his paganism was born of a heartfelt and sincere devotion to the gods. For although Julian was perfectly capable of cynical maneuvers, theatrical manipulations, and shameless propaganda to serve and strengthen his advancement among the army and people, he was also quite sincere in his religious acts. He genuinely believed the gods of Rome had saved him from death and raised him to the purple to lead the world back to the true faith. Although even those around him might have seen his conspicuous proclamations of devotion to the gods as a ploy, he meant every word of them.

———

There were a thousand things for the new emperor to do simultaneously as he gave orders for his headquarters at Nish to be moved to the imperial palace at Constantinople. But one pleasant task he made sure not to neglect was to write immediately to his friends to urge them to join him as soon as possible. He had been a lonely child and never thrived as much as he did in his later student days, when he was surrounded by like-minded intellectuals. First place among his correspondents was his teacher and old friend Maximus, whom Julian admired for both his clarity of thought and his mystical devotion to the gods: "To Maximus the philosopher: Everything is crowding into my mind at once so that I can scarcely put my words down with any coherence as one thought leaps atop another. You might call me crazed or some other appropriate word, but let me do my best to tell you what has happened, though I must first give thanks to the gods."[1]

But Julian did not write only to pagans in those first few weeks as emperor. Sometimes from a genuine respect and sometimes from a desire to stir up trouble among the enemy, he dictated letters to leading Christians of the day as well, inviting them to join him at his court in Constantinople. One of these correspondents was Basil, a fellow student from his days in Athens who was now a rising member of the Christian community. Basil had greatly impressed Julian during his brief sojourn in Athens as a serious student of Hellenism and advocate of applying the accumulated wisdom of the Greek past to Christianity. Julian wanted his court to reflect something of the intellectual diversity of the empire, even if Basil was on the wrong side of the religious divide. Basil was also a fellow admirer of and correspondent with the pagan professor Libanius, for even as a devout Christian he welcomed discourse with those who worshipped the old gods. This was the sort of Christian Julian wanted to talk to: "Although we at times refute and criticize one another with appropriate frankness, whenever possible we should treat each other with fondness as devoted friends."[2] Basil respectfully declined to come, as Julian had expected, but at least the new emperor had gone to the trouble of inviting him.

He also solicited Aetius, a mentor of his late brother Gallus. This malcontent Christian of humble origins from Antioch was so radical that even his fellow Arians thought he went too far in his desire to distinguish between God the Father and Christ. Aetius led a group known as the Anomoeans (Greek: "unlike"), who believed that Jesus was unlike and not at all of the same substance as God. The emperor Constantius was open to Arian influences, but Aetius and his followers were too radical for him, and he drove them from power within the church. Gallus, however, was drawn to this brilliant, Rasputinesque figure and welcomed him to his court when he was Caesar at Antioch. Gallus had even sent Aetius to meet with Julian twice when he heard his younger brother was showing excessive interest in Greek philosophy. Julian had assured Aetius that his own Hellenism was purely academic and that he was a faithful Christian, but he was apparently impressed by the man's intellectual abilities and perhaps even more by his potential as a troublemaker within the church. Aetius had been exiled when Gallus fell from power, but when Julian ascended the throne he was one of the first people invited to Constantinople: "I have revoked the exile of everyone banished for whatever reason by my cousin Constantius over the foolish disputes of the Galileans. But in your case I not only nullify the exile, but, since we are old acquaintances who enjoyed lively conversation together, I invite you to join me personally. You are granted the use of public transportation free of charge along with one extra horse."[3] Julian knew exactly what he was doing in showing favor to a radical like Aetius. This was the beginning of his clever strategy of dividing the different factions inside the church and pitting them against one another. Orthodox against Arians, Arian sects against each other — Julian hoped with good reason that his actions would lead to chaos within Christianity.

A final recipient of one of Julian's letters was his own uncle, his mother Basilina's brother, also named Julian, a nominal Christian at best, who was quick to see the potential advantages to reconsidering his religious loyalties. As one of Julian's few remaining relatives, he was also a welcome connection to the emperor's lost family. As someone who was not a blood relation of Constantine, Uncle Julian posed no dynastic threat. The emperor typically dictated his letters to secretaries to save time, but by the early evening in November when he wrote to his uncle from Nish, he had already busied them with other duties. In the letter he explains that the unexpected death of Constantius spared him making war on his own cousin: "The third hour of the night has just begun, and I have no secretary available to dictate to since they are all occupied, so I'm writing this with difficulty with my own hand. I am thankfully alive and by the grace of the gods freed from the necessity of either suffering or inflicting harm on anyone. By the Sun, whom of all the gods I beseeched most earnestly to help me, I swear that I never wished to kill Constantius. Truly I wanted just the opposite."[4]

His uncle would become a great supporter of Julian's and would serve him faithfully as a major government official in the eastern empire based at Antioch. Indeed, Julian's uncle would become such a fierce opponent of Christianity on Julian's behalf that church historians would remember him with the almost the same level of hatred they reserved for the nephew. The elder Julian's service was short, however, for he soon died of a painful illness, much to the delight of certain later Christians.

Julian also received many letters from well-wishers and acquaintances out of his past who were hoping to profit from their former relationships with him. Such is the nature of power, and Julian had no illusions about whether most of these correspondents would not have been equally happy were his head on a spike outside the palace, but he was gracious in his replies. One letter he received, however, was from a former teacher at Athens named Themistius, who was not seeking a favor or reward. He was a noted scholar of Aristotle and, if a Christian, certainly not a zealot of the sort who would harangue the new emperor. As Julian had read deeply in Aristotle's works on politics and the ideal ruler, Themistius simply wanted to remind the emperor that the lessons he had learned in theory were now applicable in practice. Julian appreciated the letter so much that he wrote a thoughtful reply thanking Themistius and assuring him that he would not forget his teaching: "You bade me to shake off all thought of leisure and rest so that I might prove to be a good soldier worthy of my high destiny. And you urged me to follow the example of lawgivers such as Solon, Pittacus, and Lycurgus, saying that people have a right to expect even greater things from me than from them." Julian also admits to Themistius that he wishes his life were different: "I prefer Athens to all the pomp that now surrounds me."[5] But he knows that he has little choice in the matter and that even if he could abandon the throne to return to the quiet life of a student, it is not a path he would choose. Julian had no doubt that he had been given the gift of power by the gods to rule the world with wisdom and restore their worship in an empire threatened by the incoming flood of Christianity.

It was the middle of December 361 when at last Julian and his army arrived at the gates of Constantinople. In spite, or perhaps because, of his embrace of paganism, Roman armies throughout the empire declared their loyalty to their new ruler. But before Julian had settled in the imperial palace, he began preparations for the funeral of

Constantius. Julian had no love for his cousin, but he was savvy enough to know that his legitimacy as emperor depended on his membership in the royal family. He also knew that even his most ardent supporters among the citizens of Rome wanted the office and legacy of an emperor to be treated with appropriate respect. The honor that Julian gave Constantius elevated his own standing. When the body of the late ruler arrived from Cappadocia, Julian was there to meet it, dressed in simple mourning clothing without his imperial robes. Along with members of the army escort, he helped carry the coffin with his own hands. All those present, even the people who knew how much he despised his cousin, were touched by this gesture of respect shown to Constantius. Julian attended the funeral service and stood piously as the priests commended his cousin's soul to Christ and his body was laid to rest in the family tomb beside that of Constantine and his other relatives, including Julian's own father.

The start of any emperor's reign was a perilous time. Countless administrative details demanded attention, hundreds of new appointments had to be made and a constant vigilance set for enemies, both within and outside the empire, seeking to take advantage of the inherent instability surrounding a new sovereign. But the one thing that every ruler had to guarantee was the support of the Roman legions. Without the backing of the army and its officers, an emperor's reign would be over before it began. This loyalty was won in the first place by money, but bonuses and gifts of gold were insufficient in themselves. An emperor had to show the army that it had his respect and a voice in the running of the empire. One way to do this was through the tribunals a new Augustus held to punish those who had misused power under the previous emperor.

In an effort to curry favor with the army and its generals, Julian decided to make his tribunal a strictly military court. He also yielded to pressure to hold the proceedings in Chalcedon, across the Bosporus Strait from Constantinople. Allegedly this was to remove the proceedings from the politics and intrigue of the capital, but in reality it was an opportunity to conduct the trials in secret. Julian himself did not serve as a judge, again purportedly to make the tribunal more impartial, but this was a convenient excuse to give the new emperor plausible deniability for what was coming.

Julian did not waste any time but assembled the court a month after he arrived in Constantinople. He appointed only military officers as judges, primarily men who had fought under him loyally and could be guaranteed to carry out his wishes. Chief among the judges was Salutius, who had served him so well in Gaul and had recently been appointed to the important post of praetorian prefect of the East. Mamertinus, a professional soldier and influential supporter of Julian, was also selected as a judge. Julian had such confidence in Mamertinus that he also selected him as one of the consuls for the coming year. In addition, the tribunal included Julian's cavalry officers Jovian and Nevitta, who had backed him from the beginning of his rebellion. The final two judges were Agilo and Arbitio, former supporters of Constantius. Julian chose them because they were influential military men whose selection demonstrated that the new emperor held no animosity against the soldiers who had once backed his cousin. Agilo was a German of the Alamanni tribe who had fought honorably as a Roman officer for many years and was quite willing to accept Julian amicably as ruler. Arbitio, however, was a slippery and treacherous intriguer whom Julian personally despised but whose support he needed among the pro-Constantius factions of the legions.

The trials began with accusations against two notorious intelligence officers of the court, Apodemius and Paul—the latter known as the Chain because of his ingenuous ability to link anyone he targeted to treasonous actions. These spies had made few friends in their lifetime of intrigue and were quickly condemned to death with the hearty assent of all present. Equally rapid was the condemnation of Eusebius, the leading court eunuch of Constantius, who had made many enemies on his climb up the ladder of power. The natural antipathy of soldiers for spies and eunuchs made the judgments against the first defendants easy, but further cases became more problematic. Florentius and Taurus, the governors appointed, respectively, to Italy and Illyricum to contain Julian in Gaul, were condemned under pressure from Julian despite their only crime having been loyal service to Constantius. Men whose primary failing was having a role in the downfall of Julian's brother Gallus were also found guilty, even though Julian admitted that Gallus was a cruel and inept Caesar. But the most controversial judgment at the trials of Chalcedon was the condemnation of a man named Ursulus, who had served Julian faithfully and well as his treasurer in Gaul. The army had taken a dislike to Ursulus because of insulting comments he had made about the military during a campaign in Mesopotamia years earlier. Neither forgetting nor forgiving, they demanded this good man be executed as the price of their loyalty to the new emperor. Julian, to his shame, agreed, earning reproof even from friends like Libanius. But the new emperor felt such guilt at the execution of Ursulus that he took the unusual step of returning the forfeited land and property of the condemned man to his daughter. The trials of Chalcedon are proof that Julian, like many other ambitious leaders in history, was willing to sacrifice even loyal friends for his own advancement.

Julian was by nature a frugal man who despised wastefulness and excess. In his personal life he did not indulge in sex, drinking, or gluttony, although all the temptations of the world were readily accessible to him. He was a genuine ascetic who slept on a straw mattress, hated the theater and public games, ate simply, and drank sparingly. He valued philosophy, friendship, and the gods, not wine or gold. His weakness, if it might be called that, was that he could not understand why others felt differently. He genuinely could not comprehend how anyone of goodwill and intelligence could give in, at least on occasion, to the pleasures of the flesh or be concerned with gaining wealth. This blind spot made Julian at times an unbearable prig, but combined with his desire for reform it also made him a formidable crusader in amending the massive bureaucracy that had developed under earlier emperors. Constantine's predecessor Diocletian had turned the more austere court of his day into a regal extravaganza intended to separate the emperor from the common people and evoke a sense of awe surrounding the ruler that might bring stability to the empire. This transformation of the Roman emperor into an eastern potentate was continued and enhanced by Constantine and Constantius to the point that the imperial court had become an unprecedented theatrical production. Libanius writes that there were a thousand cooks and as many butlers, with eunuchs swarming around the palace like flies around the flocks in spring. Even the military members of the court had grown soft, with common soldiers sleeping on feather mattresses, singing cabaret songs instead of marching cadences, and drinking from wine cups that were heavier than their swords.[6]

One day early in Julian's reign, a man in sumptuous robes approached him at the palace. The emperor naturally assumed that he was a high minister of state he had not yet met. When the man introduced himself as the royal barber, there to trim his hair, Julian flew into a rage and began a wholesale downsizing of the imperial staff. Large numbers of imperial slaves and eunuchs were dismissed and expelled from the palace. The fact that many of them were Christians led some later church writers to assume the expulsions were a ploy to purge Julian's staff of enemy influences, but in truth Julian removed as many pagan employees as Christians. In this matter at least, his actions were not motivated by religious feeling.

Julian followed up the execution of the prominent spies at the tribunal of Chalcedon with a drastic scaling back of the imperial secret police. He knew that some intelligence agents would always be necessary for the security of the empire and its ruler, but he had experienced at first hand the corruption and arrogance of a security apparatus that existed primarily to further its own interests, not those of the emperor. Julian also made considerable efforts during his first few weeks in Constantinople to strengthen the local governments throughout the lands he now ruled. He knew that whatever power the palace wielded, it was the town councils and local senates of the empire that accomplished the lion's share of governance in his name. These bodies not only handled the countless municipal problems — from keeping the peace to maintaining the water supply — they were also directly responsible for taxation and revenue. Many prominent residents of cities and towns deliberately avoided service as town councilors because of the onerous drain on their time and financial resources. Julian therefore established changes that would encourage leading citizens to take on municipal responsibilities, chiefly by reducing the means of avoiding them. First among these was revoking a law exempting Christian clergy from service on town councils. It might appear that Julian was opening up the avenues of Roman power on a local level to his Christian adversaries, but he was actually stripping away one of the most jealously guarded privileges of the clergy. Julian himself, however, tried to set a good example by regularly attending Senate meetings in Constantinople in person, not as the emperor but as a citizen doing his part for the city.

In his few months at Constantinople, Julian set about the daunting task of reforming and simplifying the whole governing bureaucracy with a series of imperial edicts. We know about most of them from the Theodosian Code, a comprehensive recording of Roman laws written down decades after Julian by the Christian emperor Theodosius II. Julian recognized the stabilizing influence of a well-organized bureaucracy in a government as large as the Roman Empire's, but under Constantius the number of individuals and offices required to get anything accomplished had grown out of all proportion to their usefulness. Corruption was rampant, and the privileges of the elite, including church officials, had become an expensive burden on the Roman taxpayers. Symptomatic of this was the imperial courier system, which provided horses and transport for anyone traveling in the empire on official business. By the time of Julian, not only official messengers were using the free transportation services maintained at every town and village, but also the vast network of Constantius's spies, who were said to be particularly hard on animals. Christian bishops and other churchmen had also grown accustomed to state-provided horses and services as they moved about the empire. Julian put a stop to such practices and restricted the use of the courier system to the few Roman officials who needed it. Now the clergy were forced to pay for their own horses or to walk from town to town, provoking cries of outrage from Christian leaders. Although Julian was well aware that church officials were among the chief abusers of free imperial transport, his ruling was not aimed at them specifically; he sought only to reduce the cost of the system.

Julian also ended the custom of Roman cities offering golden wreaths each year to the emperor. In recent years this had become an expensive competition to curry favor with the ruler by giving him the heaviest crown, even though many cities could ill afford such a financial burden. He also tried to ease the tax burden on average Roman citizens through revenue reforms, such as forbidding additional taxation in the provinces unless he had personally approved the increase. Much to the consternation of the imperial treasury, he scaled back taxes for many towns and forgave unpaid revenue bills of some towns which had been accumulating for years. He also opened the notoriously corrupt guild of tax collectors to prosecution by allowing them to be periodically tried and even tortured if they were found guilty of taking more than their due.

During Julian's first few months as emperor, many cities and towns from all over the empire sent representatives to Constantinople to bring whatever grievances they might have directly to the new emperor for appeal, as was their ancient right. Julian spent countless hours listening to the tedious details of local complaints and demands for justice, but even he sometimes had had enough. When a particularly loquacious embassy of Egyptians arrived in the capital to press their case for a rebate of money which they claimed had been unjustly collected over the past few decades, he announced that he was transferring the hearing across the Bosporus to Chalcedon, where he would meet them and carefully weigh their case. When the Egyptians were all on the far side of the waterway, Julian gave strict orders that no boatman was to ferry them back to Constantinople under any circumstances. He never met with them again.

Julian spent the spring of 362 at Constantinople working with enormous energy and dedication to restructure and improve the Roman government. Although these reforms were much needed and appreciated by those whom they helped, he faced fierce opposition from the entrenched interests that profited from the old system. But the remarkable result was that in a few short months Julian accomplished much of what he set out to do in repairing the broken Roman bureaucracy. Now Julian could turn his attention to the project dearest to his heart — restoring the worship of the Roman gods.

CHAPTER SIX

Against the Galileans

J ulian was a devout follower of the old gods who had firmly rejected the Christianity of his family and youth. But did he simply want to level the playing field and give paganism a fair chance to reassert itself in the empire or did he have something darker in mind from the beginning? Was Julian, that is, an advocate for the open marketplace of religious ideas or was he a budding Nero or Diocletian who would eventually outlaw Christianity and slaughter its followers? Did he plan to destroy the Christians — whom he dismissively called Galileans after the backwater homeland of Jesus — to rid the world of a faith he firmly believed was an insult to reason and a curse on humanity? The question of Julian's intentions and what he would have done given enough time on the throne has been central to both his admirers and his enemies since his own lifetime. The answer is murky, but it seems probable that his hope from the start was to weaken and eventually eliminate Christianity throughout the Roman lands. There would be no bloodbaths — at least not at first — but his ultimate goal was to press the church beneath the yoke of Roman power until it broke.

One of the first edicts Julian issued when he became emperor decreed the reopening of the temples and shrines of the Roman gods throughout the empire and the resumption of widescale animal sacrifices. His edict was perhaps an overstatement since the temples had never been formally closed nor had sacrifices been outlawed by his predecessors. But in certain localities Christian officials and bishops had shut down or at least strongly discouraged pagan worship. Nonetheless, Julian meant from the beginning to signal unmistakably to Christians that no hinderance would be allowed to the worship he clearly favored. Julian also took the unusual step of proclaiming universal religious tolerance. He assured his subjects that followers of all religious traditions—pagan, Christian, Jewish, and others—would be treated with equal respect as long as they posed no threat to the general peace and security of the empire.

The fact that these decrees were issued in the first weeks of his rule was both encouraging to the majority of imperial subjects who were still pagan and a warning to Christians that the old days of favoritism under his uncle Constantine and cousin Constantius were over. But Julian was not, at this stage, outlawing Christianity or persecuting the church. He claimed he simply wanted to give the ancient pagan religion an opportunity to flourish again and assert itself against what he considered a misguided cult invented by followers of an unremarkable Jewish rabbi. He declared that Christians would have nothing to fear from him or his imperial administration. There would be no martyrs. They would not be punished nor would their churches or scriptures be burned. They could continue to gather in worship and live their lives as before. As he wrote to Atarbius, a fellow pagan who was one of his governors in Mesopotamia: "I swear by the gods I do not want the Galileans killed or unjustly beaten or treated badly in any way. What I desire most insistently is to show preference to those who fear the gods."[1]

But in some of Julian's actions we can see the beginnings of a more troubling future. His declaration of religious tolerance also included an amnesty and right of return for all orthodox Christian leaders who had been exiled and marginalized under Constantius, who had favored Arian Christians. This was a clever move on Julian's part. As the pagan historian Ammianus would say disparagingly a few decades later, the Christians were like wild beasts who fought more viciously with each other than they ever did with pagans.[2] Rather than launch a persecution against Christians as a whole, Julian was deliberately fueling a civil war within the church to encourage the orthodox and the Arians to attack and weaken one another, leaving his own hands clean. Most notable of these pardoned orthodox exiles was Athanasius, the former bishop of Alexandria, who had been replaced by an Arian Christian leader in the city. Julian was eager to see what trouble he would stir up when Athanasius arrived back in Egypt.

Even before Athanasius returned to Alexandria, the numerous pagans of the city took their lead from the emperor and launched a series of riots against the local Christians. Scarcely a month after Julian had taken the throne and made his rejection of Christianity known, the Alexandrians murdered Bishop George, the leader of the Christian church in one of the most important towns in the Roman world. That he was an Arian and not orthodox meant little to the pagan mob. He was a Christian, and that was enough. George had been an important figure in young Julian's life during his education in Cappadocia, and his excellent library, made freely available to the prince, had given Julian a matchless window into the rich intellectual tradition of Greek philosophy and literature. The new emperor's response was not one of outrage at the murder of a prominent Roman citizen but only a mild rebuke to the crowd for taking the law into their own hands. In a letter to the Alexandrians he shamelessly pandered to the pagans of the city by casting George as an enemy to the gods who got what was coming to him: "You say that perhaps George deserved to be treated in such a fashion? I'll grant that and admit that he deserved even worse and more cruel treatment."[3]

Julian was, however, clearly more concerned about the fate of the pagan classics in George's library and made sure the treasured volumes found their way into his own collection. As for the Christian books the bishop owned, he wrote, "I wish them to be utterly destroyed. But make sure you do so with the greatest care lest any useful works be destroyed by mistake. Have George's secretary help you. Let him know that if he is faithful in the task he will get his freedom as a reward. But if he is in any way dishonest in sorting things out, he shall be put to torture."[4] Christians throughout the empire took note that in spite of Julian's outward claims concerning peaceful coexistence between pagans and Christians, the emperor would do nothing if his coreligionists hunted them down and murdered them.

Julian reinforced his militant and exclusive view of paganism through several essays published in Constantinople during the first few months of his reign. These were aimed not at Christians but rather at other schools of paganism that he found impure. The most offensive of these to him were the Cynics, a rag-tag collection of societal rebels founded by the Greek philosopher Diogenes seven hundred years earlier. Julian had a genuine admiration for traditional Cynic teachings on the rejection of wealth and comfort in the relentless pursuit of truth, as well as their general disdain for Christianity, but he had no use for the modern sort of Cynics, who in his mind were little more than greedy, illiterate layabouts masquerading as philosophers. In two surviving orations, he scolds them mercilessly for their impious behavior and compares them to the worst of the new breed of wandering Christians of his day, whom he, as well as most Christian leaders, viewed as lazy, troublesome vagabonds who knew only how to appeal to the worst instincts of the crowd they relied on for handouts: "Long ago I gave you wayward Cynics a nickname and now I think I will write it down: 'monks'—a term used by some of the impious Galileans. Like them you are for the most part men who have made small sacrifices in your lives to gain a great deal from everyone and attract a rabble of followers to give you honor and flattery."[5]

Julian catalogues all the shortcomings of the Cynics, including their straying from the noble teachings of Diogenes and their refusal to take the gods seriously. He was also appalled by their willful ignorance and disdain for education, to Julian the heart of any true effort to seek wisdom. They were even ignorant of the foundation of their own teachings: "If you had the least habit of reading books as I do—though I am a statesman busy running the affairs of a whole empire—you would know how much Alexander is said to have admired Diogenes' greatness of soul."[6]

But in his mind the Cynics' worst sin was the bad name they were giving philosophy and, by extension, his efforts to restore traditional religion. They provided ammunition to Christians, who justifiably pointed them out as examples of the failings of paganism. Julian knew that if he were going to overset Christianity he would have to make paganism a better alternative by reforming wayward movements like Cynicism.

Julian also believed the best way to defeat the church was to end division among the pagans, much as his uncle Constantine had tried to banish disunity among Christians. The followers of traditional religions had to work together in the true spirit of worshipping and honoring the gods, not squabbling with each other while the Christians happily looked on. The problem was that, like most crusaders throughout history, Julian was convinced that only his own particular religious beliefs were the right ones. But his austere form of Neoplatonism was not a belief system that had wide appeal to the pagan masses. The worship of the traditional gods of Greece and Rome had always taken a multitude of forms and had never been unified. It was not even exclusive. A good pagan might celebrate a solemn sacrifice to Zeus at a city temple in the morning followed by an afternoon visit to a shrine at a local spring and a frenzied festival honoring the goddess Cybele that same evening. The concept of a centralized set of doctrines was completely foreign to paganism. Pagans as such had no defining creeds, no universal priesthoods, and no canonical scriptures in the Christian sense. Julian was not only fighting Christianity but promoting a religion that had never existed. The fact that other pagans could not see the world in the same way he did baffled and frustrated him no end. The followers of the old gods were glad to have a non-Christian in the palace, but they wanted to be left alone to worship those gods however they thought best. Julian worked hard during the first few months of his reign to encourage paganism by legal and administrative decrees, but he was also a writer and man deeply immersed in the literary and philosophical traditions of the Greek world. He wanted to do more than command and cajole his subjects into following the old gods; he wanted to convince them through persuasion and inspiration that his spiritual vision for Rome was the right one.

One way he did this was by composing a pair of prose hymns to his favorite gods. These two short orations give us our best look into the soul of Julian and what he believed. The first, a hymn to the sun god Helios, is a creed of Julian's religious beliefs in which he attempts to lay out in sometimes tedious intellectual terms the philosophical foundations behind his religious reforms, hoping that his subjects will listen: "What I am about to say now I consider to be of the greatest importance for everyone who breathes and moves upon the earth and has a share in existence and possesses a reasoning soul and intelligence. But above all, I write it for myself."[7] He composed the work in only three days, giving it the breathless urgency so often found in Julian's writing. As in his other works, the reader gets the feeling that the young emperor had much he wanted to accomplish and little time to do so.

Julian was deeply immersed in the ideas of Neoplatonism of his day that accepted the many gods of the Greco-Roman tradition but also sought the single principle of the One or the Good that ruled over the universe, a divinity Julian and many others saw best represented in the sun god Helios. Julian had no trouble seeing this unity in the many gods who were manifestations of different parts of the whole: "I myself was blessed by the god Helios that I might be born into a family that now rules and governs the world. This god, if we may believe men of wisdom, is the common father of all humanity."[8] Zeus was the creative force of Helios, Athena was the embodiment of his intelligence, and so forth. Even gods of foreign origin such as the Persian Mithras and the Egyptian Serapis were welcomed into the Neoplatonic pantheon as universal aspects of the divine light of the cosmos. To call Julian a monotheist might be going too far, but like his contemporaries he had no problem seeing one god in the many.

Julian's hymn to Helios is a philosophical catechism for a faith that had a great appeal to intellectuals but one that he hoped would also work on a more basic level for the vast majority of his subjects, who knew nothing of and cared little for his Neoplatonic ideas. He was quite happy to have the common people of every village in the empire sacrifice an occasional pigeon to their local gods and pray for gentle rain and good health. They would follow by natural disposition and childlike innocence the wondrous ways of the many gods, who were in truth the One, while philosophers and intellectuals would seek the higher mysteries of the Good. In his mind he marveled that anyone could not see this timeless, glorious truth and celebration of life that had been perverted by the new death cult of the Christians.

In his second surviving hymn, Julian applies his mystic, philosophic view to a specific religious tradition. The cult of the great goddess Cybele originated in Phrygia in Asia Minor but was in reality the latest manifestation of the worship of a mother goddess that stretched back far into human history. The Greeks adopted this most foreign of cults into their religious world and identified Cybele with Rhea, the mother of Zeus, but also with the goddess Demeter, the keeper of the seasons and bearer of fertility to the earth, and with Aphrodite, the goddess of sex and reproduction. Cybele made her way to Rome during the Second Punic War against Carthage in spite of the very un-Roman ecstatic qualities of her worship, which included the self-castration of her priests in imitation of the self-mutilation of her consort Attis before his death and resurrection. By Julian's time the cult of Cybele was well established and respected by the Romans, though her worship had never completely lost its wild and foreign flavor.

In his hymn, Julian tries to find in the cult of Cybele a higher religious meaning and universal philosophical interpretation, all within his overarching view of the one god represented by the sun. To him Cybele represented the divine generative force just as the resurrected Attis represented the ultimate escape of the human soul from the prison of matter toward unification with the singular, immaterial Good: "Who then is the Mother of the Gods? . . . She came into being next to and together with the creator. She controls every form of life and is the cause of all generation. She brings into perfection all things that are created." Julian had no desire to denigrate the worship of Cybele and Attis as practiced by the common people: "I am aware that some reputedly wise people will call the story of Cybele an old wives' tale not to be believed."[9] But in his hymn Julian wanted to explore the deeper meaning of the myth and traditions of the Great Mother goddess. He did so in a way that would appeal to few except his fellow philosophers, but he was determined to find in all traditional religious expressions reflections of the universal paganism he hoped would defeat Christianity.

In spite of opposition from all sides, Julian set out to impose his puritanical vision of religion on the Roman world and degrade Christianity however possible. Since he rightly believed that the education of the young was at the heart of any culture, he decided to put severe restrictions on who could instruct children. In June 362, six months after taking the throne in Constantinople, Julian issued an edict that all teachers of pagan literature and philosophy throughout the empire had to be of good moral character. This in itself was harmless enough, but it was the emperor's particular interpretation of what constituted good character that turned the educational establishment upside down.

In Julian's mind, no Christian could teach the pagan philosophers since Christians did not believe the truth of them. As he reminded Christians, their master Jesus had warned repeatedly against hypocrisy among his followers. Surely they would be unwilling to instruct students in stories of the gods and teachings of pagan philosophy if they believed these were lies. And as he explained, he did not ask Christian teachers to change their beliefs. He simply gave them a choice between conversion and unemployment.

One exception Julian made in his decree against Christian teachers was a former teacher of his in Athens, Prohaeresius, whom he admired greatly in spite of his religion. Julian had kept up his correspondence with his teacher while in Gaul and had only grown in his respect for the man now that he was emperor: "Why should I not write to the excellent Prohaeresius, a man who pours forth his eloquence on the young as rivers gush their floods over the plain?"[10]

By this time the legendary rhetorician was in his late eighties, and he politely declined Julian's exemption on grounds of poor health and retired to write. He believed, moreover, that the decree would not be in effect for long, for although Prohaeresius was a devout Christian he was not above consulting pagan oracles when advantageous. When the decree had first been issued, he had asked an important Greek priest if the young emperor's reign would be long and was assured it would not be. After Julian died, Prohaeresius went back to teaching until his death at the great age of ninety-two.

Julian meanwhile continued to concern himself with the details of educating the young. Choral songs to the gods were an ancient tradition in the Greco-Roman world, and Julian wanted to make sure they were not supplanted by Christian hymns. To Ecdicius, his governor in Egypt, he wrote encouraging the prefect to support religious singing groups among the young: "If there is anything that deserves nurturing care it is the sacred art of music. Therefore select from the boys of Alexandria those sons of good birth and give them a generous allowance of grain each month along with olive oil and wine. Clothe them using funds from the state treasury."[11] As an avid reader of Plato, Julian knew the power of music to shape society and wanted to support it in every way he could against the growing influence of Christianity.

But as much as he despised the church, Julian also held a grudging admiration for its structure and practices. Almost every town in the empire had at least one active Christian congregation with priests, elders, and deacons who supervised worship and support among its members, as well as charity work among local unbelievers. As Julian wrote to a pagan priest in Galatia, "It is a shameful thing that no Jew ever has to beg and that the Galileans support not only their own poor but ours as well, while all the world sees that we don't care for our own." And again:

> When it came about that the poor were neglected and overlooked by our priests, then the impious Galileans observed this and devoted themselves to charity. Thus they have gained in numbers despite their evil ways through the credit they win for such actions. For they are just like those evildoers who entice children with a piece of cake and by giving it to them two or three times convince them to follow them. Once they are away from home and far from their friends, they cast them onto a ship and sell them as slaves.[12]

Julian knew that in a world with few social safety nets, the willingness of a religion to feed the poor and care for the sick of all backgrounds was a powerful recruitment tool. He also knew that a bishop oversaw the Christians of each town and coordinated activities with other like-minded communities across the Mediterranean and beyond through correspondence and regular meetings. Although Christianity had its divisions, it was all in all an impressive and efficient organization, one worthy of emulation in at least some of its methods.

And so in the first frenzied months of his reign, Julian set about inventing a new ecclesiastical organization for the Roman world — a pagan church with himself at its head. Emperors had in the past traditionally held the title of pontifex maximus, the chief priest of Rome, but Julian meant to imbue the office with real authority over a new religious organization dedicated to worshipping the true gods. He would appoint the priests himself and support them with the authority and financial resources of the state. One of the first priests he chose for his pagan church was a man named Pegasius, who several years earlier as a Christian bishop had given him an enthusiastic tour of the ruins of Troy. Julian suspected even then that Pegasius was a Christian by convenience rather than conviction and saw in him exactly the kind of priest he needed for his new pagan church — a dedicated lover of Hellenism who was already experienced at running a religious organization.

Julian's instructions to his new priests were clear. They were to become moral exemplars to their communities in a way Christian officials claimed to be. They were to practice charity toward strangers, care for the sick, and bury the dead with honor. They should practice modesty in all things, especially dress, though to inspire worshippers they were to wear magnificent robes when conducting holy duties. They were to avoid taverns, houses of prostitution, and other places of ill repute, especially the bawdiness of public performances: "I demand that priests withdraw themselves from the licentious surroundings of theaters and leave them to the common crowd. Therefore let no priest enter a theater or have actors or chariot drivers as friends. Let no dancer or mime ever come near his door."[13]

The priests of Julian's new pagan order were to lead lives of true asceticism and shun the empty pleasures of this world. In other words, they were to be like him. The fact that such an austere lifestyle appealed to few would-be priests seems not to have occurred to him. A number of recruits showed interest in joining the new order, but sincere devotees as opposed to favor-seekers were few. Julian's pagan church and its priesthood were a failure from the start.

As the early months of Julian's reign passed, it became clear to him that the ongoing Persian threat demanded his personal attention on the eastern frontier. The Persians sensed the empire's weakness after the death of Constantius and the ascension of an inexperienced young ruler in Constantinople. Julian was also eager to leave the capital and return to the world of war and military campaigns. He had discovered his natural talents as a warrior fighting the Germans in Gaul and was ready to face an even greater foe in the East. He was also eager to leave the stifling bureaucracy of the palace behind and return to the simplicity of army life. But the center of the Roman government was the emperor, wherever he was, and his work on a religious revolution could continue even on campaign. And so as the army gathered and the wagons were packed for the journey to Antioch and on to Persia, Julian was relentless in his efforts to bring down Christianity.

One of his more ingenious ideas for weakening the church was to form an alliance with the Jews, the very people from whom Christianity had sprung three centuries earlier. Early in his time at Constantinople, he began to court the Jews and their leaders with good wishes, financial relief, and requests for divine assistance, using language he hoped they would appreciate: "During my reign it is my fervent hope you may have security of mind and enjoy peace. Please offer earnest prayers to the Most High God, the Creator of the Universe, who has granted me the crown to rule the lands with his own righteous hand."[14]

But Julian also had a more concrete plan in mind to use the Jews in service of his own religious agenda. He knew from his youthful Christian education that Jesus had stated clearly that not one stone of the great Jewish Temple in Jerusalem would be left standing on another. This prophecy was seemingly fulfilled in 70 CE when the Roman legions sacked the city and destroyed the center of Jewish worship. The vanished Temple was a source of great sorrow to the Jews, who were allowed to visit the site only one day each year. It was also a point of pride with the Christians, who declared the ruins proof that Jesus was right.

Julian thus determined to both help the Jews as rivals to the Christians and prove false the prophecy of Jesus by rebuilding the Temple. The young emperor was no great admirer of the Jewish people, but he shared their belief that the Christian religion was a misguided faith built on false interpretations of the Jewish scriptures. In his mind, if he could form an alliance with the Jews to oppose a common enemy, both pagans and Jews would profit from the partnership.

But as was often the case with Julian, his grand plans lacked practical considerations. Foremost among these was his failure to ask the Jews whether they supported the project. The Jewish people had been taught that the Temple could be rebuilt only when the Messiah appeared. Now a pagan emperor of Rome, whose predecessors had destroyed the Temple and had murdered Jews for centuries, was putting himself in the place of the Messiah. Moreover it had been almost three hundred years since the last sacrifices were made in Jerusalem. The traditional Jewish priesthood, who were the only functionaries who could conduct such sacrifices, had been killed or scattered long ago. Jewish life and worship now centered in the synagogues dispersed throughout hundreds of communities in Roman and foreign lands. The preeminent authority in the Jewish world was no longer the high priest at the Temple in Jerusalem but the patriarch of the House of Hillel in the town of Tiberias in Galilee. Here the greatest scholars of the Jewish tradition had established themselves and were busy codifying the teachings of Talmudic Judaism that would guide Jewish life for centuries to come.

The silence that greeted Julian's plan among Jewish communities was deafening. The Jews had no wish to anger the powerful ruler of an empire which had caused so much death and destruction for their people, but to have a pagan rebuild the Temple was blasphemous and threatened to upend the whole system of rabbinic Judaism. Their lack of support did not discourage the headstrong Julian, but in the months to come the project fell apart nonetheless. Ammianus reports that balls of fire erupted from the foundations of the Temple during its early construction and injured many of the workers.[15] The disaster—which may have been the result of a random earthquake or a deliberate fire set by Christians—frightened the superstitious construction workers so badly that they refused to continue their labors. This setback, combined with the ruinous building costs and the lack of support from the Jews, prompted Julian to abandon the project even before he set off for Persia.

Events in nearby Egypt were going poorly for Julian as well. In Alexandria, stronghold of both pagan and Christian extremists in the East, the former exile and orthodox leader Athanasius had not taken up his ongoing battle against the rival Arian Christians as Julian had hoped, but instead had claimed back his title of bishop and devoted himself to spiritual war against the pagans of Alexandria. When the emperor heard of these developments, he promptly wrote to his prefect in the city and told him to throw Athanasius out of town: "I have learned that the most audacious Athanasius, so arrogant in his insolence, has seized what Christians call the episcopal throne. Citizens of the city who fear the gods are rightly upset by this. Warn him to leave Alexandria immediately. If he stays, he shall be punished most severely."[16]

Julian claimed that he had never intended his edict of universal toleration to allow Christian bishops to take up their old positions. Julian had instead hoped to ignite a civil war among Christian sects and could not comprehend why his plans were not working out as he intended. He was particularly furious at Athanasius for launching a Christian crusade in one of the leading Roman cities at the expense of his pagan revival plans: "That damned man is daring to baptize Greek women from good families while I am emperor! Let him be driven out!"[17] If Julian had known how dismissive Athanasius was of his pagan revival efforts he would have been even more angry, for the bishop was quietly assuring his followers that Julian was merely a passing cloud that would soon be forgotten.

The lack of success for his program to revive the old pagan religion was beginning to wear on Julian, prompting him to take a harsher stance. In spite of his continued claims of peaceful intent, Julian seems to have been fully aware of and even enthusiastic about the growth of violent actions against Christians in Roman lands. Riots and wholesale murder by pagan mobs erupted in many cities of the East, encouraged all the more by silence from the palace in Constantinople. Julian engaged in actions himself that can only be classed as outright oppression. In Cappadocia, he launched a full-scale persecution against the Christians of Caesarea, who were guilty only of gaining the upper hand against local pagans. Farther east in Roman Arabia, Julian had the popular bishop of Bostra driven from the city. To the Christian community of Edessa near the Persian frontier, the emperor wrote a letter reminding them that Jesus claimed the poor would inherit the kingdom of heaven — and then confiscated all their property. With scarcely a year now having passed since Julian took the throne, his true intentions regarding the Christians were becoming ever more clear.

CHAPTER SEVEN

Antioch

When Seleucus, one of the successors to Alexander the Great, founded Antioch in 300 BCE, he wanted a new city that blended the vibrant Greek world of the Mediterranean with the ancient Semitic cultures of Syria and Mesopotamia. The town quickly grew in population and became one of the largest cities in the East, with over a quarter of a million inhabitants. Greeks, Romans, Syrians, Arabs, and many others lived together in relative harmony at one of the great crossroads of the ancient world. Jews formed a substantial minority of the population and spoke, along with almost all the rest of the inhabitants, the Aramaic language Jesus had used, though Greek, Latin, and Arabic were heard as well on every street corner. In this city of many languages and cultures, Christianity had taken root early. It was in Antioch, in fact, that members of the new religion were first called Christians – "followers of the anointed one."[1]

Although Christians held a slight majority in Antioch by the time Julian took the throne, the old religions still had deep roots in the city and continued to attract many followers. Julian's own pagan mentor Libanius, one of the greatest scholars of the day, was a long-time resident and well respected by the Christians he instructed in Greek philosophy and rhetoric. Shrines to the gods were still found throughout the city, the most famous being the oracular Temple of Apollo at Daphne, on the edge of town. But even the most devout citizens of Antioch, whether pagan or Christian, generally avoided antagonizing their neighbors of different faiths. The city took pride in its cosmopolitan and tolerant attitude toward people of all creeds, focusing instead on the enjoyment of life, along with making as much money as possible.

Antioch was the natural starting point for any Roman emperor preparing to invade Persia. The Orontes River flowed out of the mountains to the east and met the sea not far from the town, making it a prime passage from the Mediterranean Basin to Mesopotamia beyond. And so in July 362, only a few months after becoming sole emperor of Rome, Julian arrived at Antioch full of excitement for the grand military adventure that he was sure lay ahead of him. The people of the city extended him a warm welcome in spite of the fact that he arrived on the same day they were weeping and wailing at the annual lamentation over the slain god Adonis (to be followed by a feast celebrating his resurrection). But Julian took the pagan holiday as a good omen and was encouraged to see such devotion to an ancient god. If he had looked more deeply he might have seen that what the crowds of Antioch really enjoyed was having a lively celebration, whether in honor of Adonis or of Christ Jesus.

Julian was busy day and night preparing his growing army for the upcoming campaign in Persia, but he was also eager to visit the shrines and temples around the city. He was especially excited to make the short journey to the Temple of Apollo at Daphne. It was a beautiful site, with flowing fountains and lush groves, that had been a major pilgrim destination for centuries. Julian's uncle Constantine had insulted the worshippers there by building a church nearby and erecting a statue of his Christian mother, Helena. He also had used cypress wood from its sacred grove to roof his new cathedral in Antioch, but Julian was certain he would still find a bustling temple to visit on Apollo's upcoming annual feast day. Instead, when he arrived with members of the city council, the place was oddly silent and empty. He thought that perhaps as emperor and pontifex maximus he was supposed to give some kind of signal, for which the celebrants were waiting, but none of his attendants could find any celebrants. At last one of his men discovered a single aged priest, who greeted the emperor with a goose brought from his own house for sacrifice. Julian was outraged and berated the local officials in attendance for caring more about their petty business concerns than for promoting and honoring the greatest god of their city. It was not a good beginning for the emperor's visit.

Things rapidly went from bad to worse. When Julian attended the hippodrome, as was expected of him, to watch the local chariot races, he was greeted by the crowd with cries of *panta gemei, panta pollou* – "Everything is plentiful, everything is expensive."[2] Antioch was suffering from runaway inflation caused by the greed of local businessmen, who had bought up the abundant grain from the surrounding provinces and were holding it in warehouses to drive up prices. The ascetic and frugal Julian once again could not comprehend why people would care more about making money than serving the public good. He first tried to remedy the situation by adding two hundred additional members to the Antiochene Senate to better manage the affairs of the city. These leading citizens, many of whom were the very merchants hoarding grain, promised the emperor they would conduct a careful study of the crisis and report back to him with due diligence. Julian was naive enough to believe them.

As the weeks went by, the people of Antioch grew increasingly hungry and were angered all the more by the army requisitioning thousands of farm animals for the emperor's sacrificial feasts. Frequent scenes of rowdy Gaulish soldiers, Julian's most loyal troops, drunk with wine and stuffed with meat from pagan festivals, only served to inflame the citizens of the town, whether Christian, Jew, or pagan. But Julian in his determination to make up for decades of neglect of the gods was oblivious to the resentment he was stirring up in the city. To him, animal sacrifices and the associated feasts were central to the worship of the gods and must therefore be encouraged, no matter what suffering they caused among his subjects.

As the summer waned in Antioch, Julian met continued resistance from the local Senate. Not only were its members ignoring him and neglecting the needs of the city, but he was finding it impossible to increase the membership of the Curia to the necessary levels. Few wealthy citizens wanted to take on a job that was notoriously draining for their own finances. He tried expanding the rolls of the Senate to include those eligible through the female line instead of simply the male, but this accomplished little. Bringing in senators from surrounding communities to serve in Antioch also failed. The local government took to bribing poor people in the marketplaces to serve in the Curia just to have men in the seats when the emperor visited the Senate House. Julian was being made a fool of by the crafty Antiochenes, who had quickly grown tired of both him and his soldiers. They were eager for him to be on his way to Persia so they could return to their corrupt and happy life.

Julian had hoped his fit of anger at the Temple of Apollo at Daphne might have had a reforming effect on worship there, but he was again disappointed. His desire to consult the oracle at the god's sacred spring was thwarted that autumn when he discovered that his own brother Gallus had ordered the bones of a Christian holy man named Babylas transferred there during his residence as Caesar. Julian learned from the remaining custodian of the temple that the voice of the offended god had been silent because the bones of the saint were polluting his grounds. He ordered the Christian remains taken back to their original grave and the spring of the god ritually purified. This only served to further inflame the Christians of the city, who lined up to escort the bones of their holy man through the city in a show of condemnation of the emperor's actions. This left Julian in an increasingly bitter mood and set the stage for what happened next.

On the night of October 22, the Temple of Apollo at Daphne burned to the ground, destroying both the building and a famous statue of the god overlaid with gold and ivory. Suspicion naturally fell upon the Christians, though there was no proof of their guilt and, in fact, some evidence that the blaze had been caused by a careless pagan philosopher who had taken shelter at the site. But Julian was having none of it. In retribution he ordered the cathedral of Antioch closed immediately and confiscated all the liturgical vessels inside, cutting the Christians off from their most sacred rituals. In revenge, Antiochenes of all religious persuasions then took to publishing scathing verses against Julian for the amusement of the populace. The tensions between the emperor and the citizens of Antioch had reached such a high that many Roman rulers would have resolved the situation with a bloody massacre. But as a man of letters, Julian decided to attack the problem in a most unusual way for an emperor.

If the populace of Antioch was going to satirize him in verse, he decided he would do them one better and write a tongue-in-cheek essay against himself mocking his best-known feature in a satirical sermon called the *Misopogon* (Beard-Hater):

> The song that I now sing has been composed in prose and contains much violent abuse. But by Zeus since the law forbids attacking others this essay is directed against the author himself. . . . For although nature did not make my face overly handsome or glowing with the bloom of youth, I decided to make matters even worse by growing this long beard of mine.[3]

He continues by attacking other of his physical features:

> If the length of my beard were not enough, the hair on my head is unkept as well since I seldom have it cut. My nails are also long and my fingers are nearly always black from writing with ink.[4]

He also chastises himself, tongue in cheek, for not indulging in the common pleasures of city life, such as plays:

> I banish myself from the theater, fool that I am, and don't allow the altar of Dionysus within my court except on the first day of the year, because I am too stupid to appreciate comedy.[5]

Chariot contests as well, the most popular entertainment of the day, hold no appeal for him:

> I hate horse races the way a man who owes money hates the marketplace, so I almost never attend them, only during the festivals of the gods. Even then I don't have the interest to stay the whole day as Constantius did or my uncle Julian or my brother Gallus.[6]

Julian continues on page after page to list his faults and short-comings. The *Misopogon* is completely unlike any surviving piece of literature we have from the hand of a Roman emperor. Whereas most rulers, such as Constantius, took great care to present themselves in the most positive way to their people, Julian took the unusual and risky tack of satirizing himself so harshly that the criticisms of others would pale by comparison and thus be dismissed. Psychologically it was a promising move since laughing at oneself is often the best way of disarming the criticism of others. But as the essay progressed, Julian could not resist lapsing into self-pity and petty complaints against the people of Antioch, pagan and Christian alike:

> This city is of one mind about me about me, for some of you hate me while the others — whom I fed! — are ungrateful. . . . I will therefore leave here and go elsewhere to a place where the citizens are of a better sort.[7]

By its end the *Misopogon* has become a tiresome litany of charges against Julian's many critics. The genuinely humorous and self-deprecating irony of its beginning collapses into the harangue of a man who believes he has been greatly wronged and grossly underappreciated. When the Antiochenes read it, they despised Julian more than ever.

In December, during the festival of the Saturnalia in Antioch, Julian, having no desire to waste his time at what he considered a frivolous party, spent a few nights composing the story of a fictional banquet of the gods and emperors of the past, including Alexander the Great, Marcus Aurelius, and Constantine. While Julian clearly admired and identified with Alexander and Marcus, he savages his uncle in a manner that was both unfair to the character of the man and deeply offensive to his Christian readers. He ends his parade of rulers with a befuddled Constantine searching the banquet hall for the divinity he most desires, finding her in the goddess Pleasure. This personification of hedonism dresses him in fine robes and leads him to the god Incontinence, who embodies the emperor's lack of self-control. Alongside Incontinence sits none other than Jesus, preaching to the crowd: "Let him who is a seducer, a murderer, sacrilegious and notorious in sin, approach me without fear! With the waters of baptism I will bathe him and make him new. If he sins a second time, let him simply smite his breast and pound his head and I will make him clean all over again."[8]

Such a mockery of their savior further enraged the Christian community of Antioch and offended even the thoughtful pagans of the city, who saw the emperor hurting their own standing with his disdainful tirades against the church and its founder.

But Julian was saving his most biting critique of Christianity for last. Before he left for Persia, the emperor was determined to put down in writing a careful refutation of Christian doctrine: "I think it would be expedient for me to set forth for everyone everywhere the reasons I am convinced that the stories of the Galileans are fictions composed by wicked men."[9]

In a lengthy treatise titled *Against the Galileans,* he tried to refute the Christian idea that Jesus was the fulfilment of prophecies found in the Hebrew Bible. He was convinced, as were many critics before him, that the writers of the Gospels had twisted the passages of the Hebrew prophets to fit their own vision of a supposed Messiah: "The words that were written concerning Israel, Matthew the Evangelist plainly transferred to Christ. In doing so he took advantage of the simple fools among the Gentiles who believed."[10]

Unlike most of the pagan apologists before him, Julian was a particularly formidable opponent of the Christians because he knew their scriptures and teachings so well. The long years he had spent studying Christian theology with dedicated teachers were now turned full force on the religion of his childhood. Julian's treatise against Christianity is merciless in its attack, perhaps influenced by the miserable time he was having in Antioch when he wrote it: "The Christian Gospels have nothing divine in them, but instead make use of that childish and foolish part of the human soul that loves fables. In doing so they have induced people to believe that the monstrous tale of Christ is true."[11]

Julian begins by noting, as Cicero and others did before him, that all humans yearn by nature for the divine and that different people pursue this longing in different ways. He admires some of what the Jews have done with their religion, though he holds it as distinctly inferior to the traditional Greco-Roman worship of the many gods. But the Christians, he says, have fallen far short of even what the Jews have achieved and have the audacity to think that theirs is the one, true doctrine from heaven.

Julian never argues that the stories of the gods, such as Kronos swallowing his children, are true in a literal sense, rather than metaphors meant to teach people a higher lesson. But the Christians, he claims, are unable to make this leap and thus tie themselves in knots trying to explain how every word in their own scriptures and those they stole from the Jews are reported facts of history. He freely admits to lessons that can be learned from the story of Adam and Eve, but happily highlights illogical points in the story if read literally, such as the fact that serpents cannot speak. He also questions human nature as supposedly designed by the Hebrew God: "Isn't it strange that God should deny to the humans he designed the power to distinguish between good and evil? What could be more useless for people than not being able to tell the difference between right and wrong?"[12]

Julian continues for the rest of the work that has survived to lay out a devastating and angry case against the basic beliefs of the Christians, freely quoting Plato and other Greek philosophers alongside the words of the Hebrew scriptures and the New Testament to prove to his readers that the church was a house built on sand.

Against the Galileans makes a strong case and would stand as an even more convincing argument against Christianity if it had survived antiquity intact. Unlike most of Julian's works, it was lost, most likely through deliberate Christian suppression. But we are able to read a portion of it today because some seventy years after Julian's death, a bishop of Alexandria named Cyril decided to write a point-by-point refutation of Julian's arguments. In doing so he quotes extended passages of Julian's work, thus preserving them for later readers. Although Cyril clearly edits out some of the most offensive remarks about Jesus, his text is regarded as generally faithful to Julian's original. Almost all the fragments I have quoted are from the first of the three books of Julian's treatise, but this is enough to give us an idea of the erudition and power of the work. Indeed, one of the reasons Cyril and other church fathers were determined to refute *Against the Galileans* was that it had caused so many Christians to question the truth of their own religion.

When spring arrived in Antioch, Julian was only too happy to leave behind the city that had treated him so badly. His preparations for the campaign against Persia were complete, and the army was ready to move east into Mesopotamia for the greatest war of Julian's short reign. It was only at the end of his stay that some of the leading citizens of Antioch began to worry that they might have pushed the emperor too far. Even a ruler as restrained as Julian could become vengeful against a people who had offended him. Julian would not have been the first Roman emperor to make a city pay dearly for insulting behavior. Crowds of citizens hoping to make a good parting impression accompanied him out of the gates of Antioch cheering him on and wishing him well in his war against the Persian enemy. His mentor Libanius pleaded with Julian to forgive the unkindness of his fellow citizens and to remember that they were already suffering greatly from shortages of food. But in spite of their pleas, Julian wanted nothing more to do with Antioch. He declared that on his return from Persia he would not pass through the town again but would make Tarsus in Asia Minor his eastern headquarters in the future. He would not punish the city, but he had no desire ever to return to the cursed place. The city would enjoy no imperial favor and receive no benefits or attention from him in the future. Julian had turned his eyes away from Antioch to the glorious victories he was sure lay ahead in Persia.

CHAPTER EIGHT

Persia

As a boy Julian had eagerly read stories of the campaigns of Alexander the Great and his conquest of the mighty Persian Empire. Alexander had set out from Macedonia and marched eastward all the way to India with his army, turning back only when his weary soldiers refused to go any farther. Now the young Roman emperor, happy to leave the troublesome citizens of Antioch behind, was ready to set off on his own Persian conquest. He had no plans to march to the Indus River; he wanted only to take Mesopotamia back from the Persians. But if the army were victorious and the gods were favorable, who could say what might happen?

Julian had good reason to be confident. He had repeatedly fought the Germans, some of the toughest warriors in the ancient world, and never lost a battle. The Persians were in disarray at the time and were clearly worried to see a Roman emperor on their borders. They had sent word to Antioch that they wished to negotiate a suitable peace, but Julian had curtly dismissed them with the message that he would be seeing them soon in their own capital of Ctesiphon. Julian was also thrilled to be going into war with his closest friends and advisers, the Neoplatonic philosophers Maximus and Priscus, intellectuals and followers of the traditional gods who he believed would offer him sound military advice—or at least raise the level of conversation around the emperor's dinner table. He also brought his old friend the physician Oribasius, another pagan voice, to help balance out the disgruntled Christians among his officers.

For Julian had serious problems with his army. Although he had brought many loyal pagan troops with him from Gaul, most of the soldiers under his command in the East were unfamiliar with him as a general and, more important, were Christians. Some were willing to set aside religion for the sake of Persian spoils, but most were unhappy with the emperor's aggressive attempts to convert them or at least his disregard for their religious beliefs. For his part, Julian saw the renewal of the Roman army under the banner of the old gods as a key element of his overall religious reforms. He was determined to purge the overt Christian elements from the legions, by bribes if possible, by threats and punishment if necessary.

He offered gold to soldiers who would sacrifice to the gods, and more than a few took his gifts, but there were many sincere Christians in the army who were deeply offended by the emperor's actions. They were brave soldiers who had bled for Rome under the banner of Christ and were willing to serve a pagan emperor loyally if their faith were granted respect. But Julian was a man of absolutes who believed he was on a heavenly mission to purge the Roman Empire and its army of the impious Christians and their offensive religion. He commanded the Christian legions to remove the Chi-Rho symbol of Christ from the standards they had marched and fought under since the days of Constantine the Great. He also ordered them to sacrifice to the gods, as generations of soldiers before them had done stretching back to the foundation of the Roman Republic. Some complied, but the standard bearers of two key units,

Juventinus and Maximinus, would not yield to the wishes of the emperor under any circumstances, and he had them beheaded. They would one day become celebrated martyrs of the church, but the immediate effect was a chill that descended across the army units, Christian and pagan alike. Even worshippers of the old gods warned Julian that he was going too far and too fast in his obsessive desire to cleanse the army of Christian influences. It was then reported that a few members of the emperor's own elite guard were planning to assassinate him, leading to the exile or execution of several guardsmen. The omens from the gods were taken repeatedly by the army's Etruscan soothsayers, but the results were clearly unfavorable for the invasion. Nonetheless, in spite of the pall that had fallen over the army, Julian was determined to go forward.

On March 5 in the year 363, the Roman army of the emperor Julian marched out of Antioch and headed east toward Persia. His force was enormous, with perhaps eighty thousand men under the now pagan banners of the legions. The men crossed over the coastal highlands of Syria, then down into the low hills of northern Mesopotamia to the ancient trading center of Beroea, modern Aleppo, near where Alexander had entered the valley of the Tigris and Euphrates rivers during his own conquest of Persia more than six hundred years earlier. The city and indeed the whole of northern Mesopotamia had been Roman for several centuries but had suffered from being on the front lines of the ongoing conflict with Persia. Although it was largely a Christian town, Julian offered a white bull to Zeus on the acropolis of Beroea and lectured the assembled city fathers on the superiority of the pagan religion of their ancestors. As he discouragingly wrote to Libanius, he persuaded none of them to change their faith. As he also complained to his mentor, the exhausting paperwork involved in being a Roman emperor never ceased, even when he was at war against Persia: "As for the number of letters and papers I have signed, why should I try to add them all up? For these follow me everywhere like my shadow."[1] Little did Julian know, but this letter to Libanius would be the last thing he would ever write.

From Beroea the army moved northeast to Batnae, where the city councilors, having heard of events in Beroea, met the emperor with conspicuous sacrifices in an attempt to win his favor. But Julian was in no mood to be appeased. He scolded the local senators, saying that true and pious followers of the gods do not make a show of devotion. Such criticism left the town confused and angry at an emperor who seemed impossible to please. He then moved on to the city of Hierapolis, a town famous for its sanctuary to the great Syrian fertility goddess Atargatis. He was drawing near to the Euphrates, where he made preparations to meet the fleet his engineers were building to sail down the river. But instead of waiting for the boats to be ready, Julian made a sudden dash across the northern plains of Mesopotamia to the Assyrian city of Carrhae, ancient Harran, the very town at which Abraham had tarried on his way to the promised land of Canaan. It was also the site of one of Rome's greatest defeats, when in 53 BCE Crassus, an ally of Julius Caesar, and his army of twenty thousand Roman soldiers had been killed in a battle against the Persians. Julian had no interest in playing tourist; instead he was there to worship at the ancient temple of the moon god Sin. Ammianus records in a later story that Julian took his maternal cousin Procopius with him and gave him a purple cloak, instructing Procopius to seize the throne if he himself should die in Persia. It is most unlikely that this story is true, though Procopius did stage a failed coup a few years later. It is possible, however, that Julian was beginning to have genuine doubts about the wisdom of his Persian campaign. Ammianus reports that at Carrhae the emperor had fearful nightmares. As was discovered later, on the same night Julian was having his dreams, the Temple of Apollo on the Palatine Hill in Rome burned to the ground. It was a dread omen in the eyes of the pagan historian Ammianus, revealing that the gods were not in favor of Julian's war. He also records that Salutius, Julian's mentor in Gaul and a man the emperor greatly respected, had urged him to turn back from Persia. Salutius warned that as a practical matter it was too early in Julian's reign to undertake such a major campaign and that he should instead focus on religious and economic reforms within the empire. He stated bluntly that the end result of the war would be Julian's death. But once again, the determined emperor did not listen.

At this point Julian unexpectedly sent some thirty thousand men, at least a third of his army, east into the mountains of Media to attack this Persian province and lure the Persian forces away with the help of his ally Arsaces, king of Armenia. This mountainous country in northern Mesopotamia had long been a buffer state between Rome and Persia. The Armenians had in the past frequently played the two major powers off against each other to their own advantage, but Arsaces had generally supported Rome, especially after Constantius had given him the daughter of an important Roman governor in marriage to seal their alliance. Armenia had officially adopted Christianity even before Constantine, but Julian was willing to overlook religious affiliations if it served his military purposes. His main concern was that Arsaces send his army to support Julian's own. Julian had written to him earlier, as he was leaving Antioch, "Make haste, Arsaces, to meet the battle line of the enemy and quickly arm yourself against the madness of the Persians."[2]

Sending thirty thousand of his men into Media to temporarily join with the army of Arsaces was a risky move, but Julian gave the Roman commanders of the expedition strict orders to return quickly to meet the main body of the legions when they approached the Persian capital. He knew that if they were delayed, the main body of the Roman army would be in trouble deep in the heart of Persian territory.

Julian then tried to throw off the Persian scouts following his army by leading his men on a rapid march east before veering back to the Euphrates River at Callinicum. Both these maneuvers were sound if unusual strategies based on the same misdirection he had employed so successfully in Gaul, but they depended on the Persians being gullible enough to fall for them. What Julian failed to appreciate was that the Persians were highly professional and calculating soldiers long familiar with fighting throughout the vast, open plains of Mesopotamia. They were not easily intimidated by an emperor who had learned the art of battle warring against brave but erratic Germans in the dark forests of Europe. They knew that if they could draw Julian far enough south into unfamiliar country, away from his supply lines and reinforcements, they could wear him down, envelop his army, and crush him. All they needed was time and patience.

When Julian returned to the Euphrates at Callinicum, he found his fleet waiting for him. The armada was huge, with more than a thousand ships filled with food, weapons, and siege supplies, along with special boats designed for bridging rivers. The Romans had never been so well prepared to wage war in Mesopotamia. Julian also gained more allies in Callinicum when the leaders of the local Arab tribes offered to join his fight against the Persians. The Romans knew their loyalty would last only as long as the legions seemed likely to win, but Julian welcomed the help of a people who knew the land well.

The sources for Julian's Persian campaign unfortunately be-

come limited and sometimes contradictory at this point. It is difficult to know precisely where the army went and, even more important, why the emperor did what he did. Julian was meticulous in
recording events, but his own accounts of the final weeks of his life
are lost. Even so, his overall plan is clear. The fleet would sail down
the wide Euphrates several hundred miles to the Persian capital of
Ctesiphon while the army marched along on the roads beside them.
Julian made good use of his pontoon boats and built a bridge over
the Khabûr River, which flows into the Euphrates from the mountains of Anatolia. The Romans had now crossed into Persian territory. Once across, Julian had the bridge dismantled so that no one
in his army might think of turning back.

Soon the legions marched past the tomb of the Roman emperor
Gordian III, a ruler who had died over a century earlier at only nine-
teen years of age while also advancing on the Persian capital. His
war had ended in failure and death, an omen which could not have
failed to send a shudder down Julian's spine as he gazed at the monu-
ment. He quickly rode on to the deserted city of Dura-Europus, a
frontier town that had been evacuated and abandoned a century
earlier by the Persians. It was an empty shell in Julian's time with
only the wind left to blow through the lonely streets, but in its day
it had been a lively trading post with a vibrant mixture of Greek
and Mesopotamian culture founded by the successors to Alexander
the Great. Jews had lived peacefully alongside Arabs and Greeks,
while a thriving Christian community had built a church decorated
with colorful frescoes of biblical scenes, not far from a Jewish syn-
agogue and a temple to the pagan god Mithras. Ammianus wrote
that Julian's soldiers killed a large lion there, which the soothsayers
said foretold the death of a king.[3] Julian, with the encouragement
of his philosopher friends, chose to believe it presaged the end of
the Persian ruler Shapur, not himself, but his men were not so sure

and began to grow more concerned as they moved ever deeper into Persian lands. A mighty clap of thunder and bolt of lightning from a clear sky one sunset soon afterward upset them further. In an age when the most rational of men were far more superstitious than in later centuries, wonderous signs from the heavens were taken seriously and could change the course of a war. The fact that Julian kept interpreting these signs favorably against the advice of his professional priests was not at all comforting to his soldiers.

But the journey into enemy territory had been successful so far and continued to go well, at least for a time. At Anatha, a fortified town on an island in the Euphrates, the inhabitants quickly surrendered under promise of peaceful resettlement in Roman territory. Among the delegation was a frail and elderly man who saluted the emperor and identified himself as a Roman soldier who had been left behind injured almost seventy years earlier by the Roman emperor Galerius during an earlier campaign in Mesopotamia. He had recovered and chosen to remain behind, taking native wives and becoming part of the community. Julian was astonished to meet this living link to the past and gratefully sent him on his way with the other residents of Anatha to live out his remaining days in Roman lands.

A few days later the legions came to the river town of Thilula, which Julian agreed to bypass after the inhabitants declared their neutrality in the war. He could have taken the settlement but did not want to get bogged down in an endless series of sieges as he moved toward the capital. The prize was Ctesiphon and the Persian king Shapur. Julian knew that if he could capture one or both of them, he would be ruler of Mesopotamia all the way to the Persian Gulf.

Events in the coming days cheered both Julian and the army. At Ozogardana, the inhabitants fled before the legions arrived, enabling Julian's army to easily loot and destroy the empty city. The Roman emperor Trajan had erected a tribunal platform there more than two centuries earlier. As Julian stood atop the structure built by his famous predecessor, he must have been encouraged, thinking that he was on the same glorious path as a ruler who in his day had soundly defeated the Persians.

The Roman army was now drawing near to the Persian capital at Ctesiphon. Not far from the city, Julian and his men came to the King's River, which connected the Tigris and Euphrates. Along the waterway were several key towns taken quickly by the Romans, including Pirisabora, which the troops looted and then burned. Soon after this a squadron of Roman cavalry on a reconnaissance mission was ambushed and killed by the Persians, who captured the prize trophy of a Roman standard, something Roman soldiers were expected to protect at the cost of their lives. Julian himself commanded the force that assaulted the enemy to retaliate. He was so upset by the shameful affair that he executed the remaining officers, and the surviving soldiers were forced to undergo the rare penalty of decimation, in which they chose lots, and one out of ten (*decem* in Latin) was then executed. Julian's reaction was so extreme that it may reveal a detachment on his part from the increasingly perilous situation the army was in as they moved farther from Roman territory. The harsh punishment of their fellow soldiers helped feed the growing discontent throughout the legions.

Julian was facing serious problems within his army. The Christians were still seething over their treatment at the hands of an aggressively pagan emperor, and all the soldiers were complaining about the poverty of spoils in the poor river towns they had taken. A bonus payment from the emperor was deemed inadequate, leading to a near mutiny among the troops. Julian calmed the men temporarily with the promise of the rich treasures awaiting them at Ctesiphon, at which they soon arrived.

Julian provided a distraction from recent events by holding athletic games just below the walls of the Persian capital. Aside from entertaining his troops, it was a clever psychological ploy against the Persian army waiting behind the walls. If they could stage cavalry races as the troops of Shapur looked on from atop the city ramparts, how worried could Julian and the Romans be?

In truth, very worried. The large army that Julian had sent into Media at the beginning of the campaign had failed to make the expected rendezvous at Ctesiphon, leaving the emperor with a third fewer men than he had counted on to attack the fortified capital. More ominous, he received word that the bulk of Shapur's vast army, which had been fighting elsewhere in the empire, was now approaching the city. Ammianus, who was present as a young soldier at Ctesiphon, recorded that the armor of the thousands of Persian cavalry gleamed in the sun and their battle elephants looked like moving hills as they positioned themselves around the legions.[4] Julian's German and Gaulish soldiers had never seen anything like the beasts that were now facing them, and they were terrified. Julian nonetheless launched an attack on the Persians and took them by surprise, driving some behind the walls of the city, but he failed to follow through on his small victory. It was as if the heart had gone out of the emperor. He had never faced a fortified city like Ctesiphon before, and he knew that a successful siege was all but impossible given the towering walls and plentiful supplies in the town. And now even more Persian soldiers were on the way. He and his men would probably be caught between the Persian army and the walls of the city, easy prey for the eager soldiers of Shapur.

Julian's veteran officers warned him that the legions were facing a critically dangerous situation and advised him to break off the siege of the city and escape back to Roman territory before it was too late. Julian saw his dreams of conquest slipping away. As his old schoolmate and adversary Gregory would smugly write, at that point, "like sand slipping from beneath his feet or a mighty storm bursting on a ship, things began to go black for Julian."[5]

Heartbroken and dispirited, Julian reluctantly agreed to retreat. He tried to put the best face on the situation for the army, framing it as a successful punitive campaign deep into Persian territory, but even the lowliest Roman soldier could see that in this rapid turn of events they had lost the war.

It was at this point that Julian carried out one of the most inexplicable actions of his entire military career — he ordered all the Roman supply ships burned. The whole fleet of a thousand ships was put to the torch in the sight of both the Roman army and the Persians in the city. Admirers of Julian in years to come would try to defend this bizarre move, but their arguments are unconvincing. Some said that the ships would have been too hard to sail back upriver against the current, while others claimed the action was to prevent lazy soldiers from sleeping on the boats while their comrades were forced to march alongside them. But neither is a convincing reason for why Julian would abandon the means to transport his crucial supplies, most notably because ships had been sailing up the slow-moving rivers of Mesopotamia for millennia. What seems more likely is that Julian had fallen for the oldest trick in war when a Persian, claiming to be a helpful ally to the Romans, offered to lead the army on a shortcut away from the rivers safely back to their borders. Why such an otherwise intelligent man as Julian would put the fate of his army in the hands of one dubious traitor is baffling, but one cannot help but wonder if he felt the gods had miraculously provided him with a means to save his army and his own reputation. Ammianus claims that Julian realized his mistake and tried to put out the flames as the fleet burned, but it was too late.[6] Julian and his army of tens of thousands of men were now desperately short of supplies deep in enemy territory. If Julian, who had read Xenophon's *Anabasis* describing a similar situation faced by a Greek army centuries earlier, thought that it would be easy to escape with a relentless and vengeful Persian army on his heels, he was about to discover how wrong he was. The generals of Shapur carefully laid their plans to destroy the Romans. They began by burning all the crops in the lands the legions would have to march through. With no supply ships and no way to live off the land, this scorched-earth policy guaranteed that the Romans would soon begin to starve.

Julian's retreat with his beaten army through the barren plains of Mesopotamia was the greatest disaster of his short but otherwise admirable military career. He had hoped the gods might carry him to glory like Alexander, but now he would be fortunate to get his men out of a terrible situation alive. He also knew that emperors had recovered from defeat before, but their reputations had been damaged and their reigns were often short. Soldiers and citizens expected victory and rich spoils from war, not inglorious defeats. For Julian the failure was even more severe because he had tied the momentum for his pagan revival to the favor of the gods in the war against Persia. Now he had nothing to show for his efforts. It did not take long for Christians across the empire to see vindication in Julian's defeat. Surely the Christian God had shown that he was supreme and even apostate emperors must bow before him. If the war against Persia had been a grand trial of faith by combat, Julian and the pagans had lost.

The Persians were not going to let Julian and his army move back across their border unhindered. As the days and nights went by, the cavalry of Shapur and his elephant corps kept up constant attacks on the demoralized legions. The Roman soldiers had abandoned all hope of winning. Julian tried his best to encourage and inspire them, but even he had lost his enthusiasm for fighting.

Julian was still a Roman emperor, however, and not one to abandon his responsibilities or neglect to face danger alongside his men. On the afternoon of June 26, 363, he received word from messengers that the Persians had again attacked the legions in the rear of his marching army. Julian rushed to gather his weapons and rode at speed back to repulse the assault. In his haste he neglected to put on the heavy mail coat he had taken off earlier in the rising heat of the day. He reached the rear lines just as the Persian cavalry and elephants again hit his men. The legions rallied at the sight of their emperor fighting among them and pushed the Persians back into flight. Julian was quick to seize this small victory and rode forward ahead of his guards into the fray, encouraging his men to follow.

It was now, when he was alone chasing the Persians, that death found him. The fatal spear grazed his arm and pierced his ribs before plunging deep into his liver. Julian tried to pull it out with his own hands, but it had gone too deep. He fell from his horse while his men tried too late to protect him from the Persians. He was quickly taken back to the Roman camp, where his friend the physician Oribasius did his best to ease the pain, but it was as clear to Julian as to everyone present that he would not survive the night. Ammianus records that Julian spent his final hours in the same manner as Socrates:

> He engaged with Maximus and Priscus in a calm and careful discussion concerning the immortality of the soul. Suddenly the wound in his side opened wide and the flow of blood began to block his breathing. He asked for a drink of cold water, then passed away quietly in the darkest hour of the night.[7]

Julian

At thirty-two years of age, the same age as Alexander the Great at his death, the emperor Flavius Claudius Julianus died on a battlefield in Persia far from home. One might hope that he found in death something of the final peace he longed for in his hymn to the god Helios:

> When fate wills at the proper hour, may I have the most gentle exit from this life and ascend to be with him, if possible, to abide and be with him forever.[8]

CHAPTER NINE

Legacy

Before his body was cold, rumors began to spread among the army that it had not been the Persians who killed Julian but one of his own men. Suspicion naturally fell on the Christians, many of whom would be eager in years to come to take credit for slaying an enemy of God who had made war on the true faith. Julian's mentor and friend Libanius asserted that he had been murdered by a follower of Jesus who believed he was acting as an agent of God. But with the confusion of battle on a distant plain long ago, no one can be sure what really happened or who it was who sent the fatal spear into Julian's side. All that is certain is that Julian was dead and with him his dream of restoring the glory of the ancient gods of Rome.

After the death of Julian, the only concern of his generals was to make it back to Roman territory safely. But first they had to choose a new emperor. Julian had no heirs, his wife, Helena, having died childless, and there was no one left alive in the family of Constantine to take up the mantle of rule. With the need for a military commander of imperial power to manage the army's retreat, Julian's successor would have to be someone present on the Persian campaign. Julian's maternal cousin Procopius was there, but he was related by blood only through Basilina and so had no solid claim to the throne, even if the generals had been impressed by him, which they apparently weren't.

The competing factions among the military leaders, Christian and pagan alike, each wanted its own candidate elevated to the purple and argued bitterly throughout the next day and night. All the factions could at least agree that Julian's wise adviser Salutius was the best man for the current crisis. He was an experienced command officer and accomplished administrator who had served as Julian's mentor since the young Caesar's days in Gaul. Although a pagan, he was widely respected by the Christians in the army and by the royal court in Constantinople, since he had no desire to force his beliefs on others. But Salutius straightway refused to take the title of Augustus. He claimed age and poor health as his reasons, but it seems more likely he saw the throne as a curse rather than a blessing. There was no time for prolonged debate with the Persians constantly attacking them, so the military council selected Flavius Jovianus — the cavalry officer Jovian — who was unremarkable but reliable and a senior staff officer the same age as Julian. His most outstanding quality was that he was quite tall.

Jovian was a Christian but not a fanatic, with interests tending more toward women and wine than prayer. He had served in the household guard under Constantius and had escorted the body of the previous emperor back to Constantinople for burial, an act that gave him some recognition to the Roman public. As lacking as Jovian might have been in intellect and vision, he had a very well-connected father and father-in-law, who had served the empire in high office and promised to smooth his way at the imperial court. Both the power brokers in Constantinople and the generals in Persia wanted and needed a return to social and religious stability throughout Roman lands. Julian's uncompromising pagan zeal appealed to few and would gladly be forgotten by all.

Jovian immediately appointed Salutius to negotiate a peace deal with the Persians. With constant attacks still raging and the legions panicking, even the experienced general had little leverage to press the Roman case. In only four days he had negotiated a peace treaty that gave the Persian ruler Shapur everything he wanted. In exchange for safe passage, the Romans surrendered the eastern regions of Mesopotamia they had fought so hard to secure along the upper Tigris, including the key frontier city of Nisbis. This decimated Roman trade and tax revenues as well as greatly weakening the Romans' military position on the eastern frontier. The Romans also agreed not to interfere in the affairs of Armenia, long a key ally on the Persian borders. The one-sided treaty was a complete capitulation and a devastating blow to Rome, one that would be felt for generations to come.

This left the new emperor Jovian in a terribly weak position at the start of his reign. He would have to assume the throne draped in the pall of defeat from losing a war he had not started. He did his best to put a good face on the situation — literally in the case of quickly minting new coins to distinguish himself from Julian. His image was clean-shaven and framed with Christian symbols. He also dispatched letters throughout the empire trying desperately to convince the Roman people that the Persian campaign was somehow a victory in spite of the death of an emperor and the loss of so much territory. But he convinced no one. He managed to lead the defeated legions out of Mesopotamia and back to Antioch, where the fickle citizens treated him even more badly than they had Julian. The Antiochenes wrote scathing anonymous pamphlets against him and shouted to his face in the hippodrome that he should have died in Persia. Fate as well as the Roman people were not kind to Jovian. His reign was short and undistinguished. Within a year he would be dead in Asia Minor by asphyxiation from the fumes of a charcoal stove.

Julian's body was granted the battlefield honors due a Roman emperor, and his remains, preserved in honey, were transported from the site of his death in a decorated cart alongside the army on its dispirited retreat. The Christian historian Ephrem, a native of Nisbis, saw the funeral procession of "the accursed one" Julian pass through his city just before the Persian standard was raised over the walls.[1]

In death Julian was treated no better by the people of Antioch than he had been while still alive. The Christian and pagan citizens of the town danced in the streets and acted as though the demise of the emperor were a cause for celebration. The fact that the Persian border was now uncomfortably closer to their city seemed not to have occurred to them. Antioch was the last place Julian would have wanted for his tomb, so the funeral procession continued on to Tarsus, a city much more to his taste. Although it was the hometown of the apostle Paul, it was also a sophisticated university city with a deep intellectual tradition.

So Tarsus came to hold the bones of Julian, perhaps because Jovian was in a hurry to get back to Constantinople to secure power. The funeral was short and simple, as Julian would have wanted. An inscription on stone, perhaps composed by Libanius, was placed above his tomb: "Here lies the body of Julian, who fell by the waters of the swift Tigris. He was a good king and a mighty warrior."[2]

There were plans in the years following to remove Julian's remains from Tarsus to Constantinople, but it was not until three hundred years later, under a Byzantine emperor, that his body found its final resting place. It was then his bones were taken from Tarsus to the Church of the Holy Apostles in Constantinople, the very place where Julian had celebrated the funeral of Constantius, to be entombed beside the other members of the royal family, including his own father. For Julian it surely would have seemed a final, bitter defeat to be buried for eternity in a Christian church.

At the death of Julian, most of the people who lived across the vast Roman Empire were pagans. Sacrifices were still made to the gods in thousands of temples and shrines from Syria to Britain. Traditionalists such as the senator Symmachus in Rome fought valiantly in the decades to come against the new religion, but with the end of the last pagan ruler to sit on the throne of Rome, everyone knew that the battle was lost. Even Julian's old friend and mentor Libanius could see the handwriting on the wall: "The Christians have quenched the sacred flame and stopped the joyful sacrifices. They spurn and overthrow the altars of the gods. These people have closed, demolished, or profaned the temples and shrines so that they are now the dwelling place of prostitutes. Reverence for the gods is gone. In their place we have inherited a dead man's tomb."[3]

All the ancient oracles of the gods were gradually abandoned or turned into churches, the mystery religions that inspired hope and awe among their followers dwindled away, and the ancient pagan schools of philosophy in Athens and elsewhere became empty ruins. In the 380s, the Christian Roman emperor Gratian declined the ancient title of pontifex maximus because of its pagan origins and removed the Altar of Victory from the Senate house. In 391, the emperor Theodosius issued a decree closing the remaining temples and shrines to the gods and forbade all pagan worship. With this final act, the Roman Empire became irrevocably Christian and brought about the end of paganism that Julian had feared. The voices of the gods were now silent.

The memory of Julian did not die, though for many centuries history was not kind to him. In the European Middle Ages he became a symbol of godless evil in literature and art. Stories were invented of brave Christians who refused to renounce their faith during his reign only to be cruelly martyred. A church was even built in Rome to honor a pair of fictional saints who were loosely based on the story of two malcontent Christian soldiers executed by Julian before the Persian campaign. Other imaginary martyrs were to follow as the years went by. Stories of the apostate emperor appear far and wide throughout Christian Europe, even making their way into Norse sagas.

Not until the Renaissance did Julian again find champions. The writings of the Latin historian Ammianus had circulated since classical times and thinkers of a new age began to read of Julian in them with fresh eyes. Michel de Montaigne recognized him as a gifted Roman leader and a philosopher of true virtue. English Protestant reformers, oddly enough, saw Julian as a kindred spirit in their fight against the tyranny of the Roman church. The French philosopher Voltaire also discovered in Julian an ideal ruler and wrote of him in a way that profoundly reshaped European views of the emperor in a positive light. The historian Edward Gibbon in his *Decline and Fall of the Roman Empire* took up Voltaire's cause and backed it with an unmatched knowledge of Roman history to complete Julian's makeover from pagan villain to sympathetic Enlightenment hero. In the twentieth century, the Alexandrian Greek writer Constantine Cavafy and the American novelist Gore Vidal continued to celebrate Julian as a romantic figure fighting a brave but hopeless battle against the suffocating power of the church.

Whether we agree with these modern interpretations or not, it is hard not to admire the spirit of Julian in his struggle for what he believed was right. Although he ultimately failed because of his unwillingness to compromise and his impossibly high standards, he was nonetheless one of the most remarkable figures of the ancient world.

Chronology

Genealogy

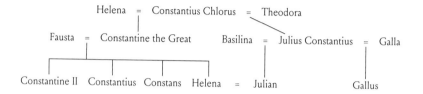

Helena = Constantius Chlorus = Theodora

Fausta = Constantine the Great   Basilina = Julius Constantius = Galla

Constantine II   Constantius   Constans   Helena = Julian   Gallus

Notes

CHAPTER 1. A CROSS IN THE SKY

1. Pliny the Younger, *Letters* 10.97.

CHAPTER 2. THE EARLY YEARS

1. Libanius, "Funeral Oration over Julian," *Selected Orations*, 18.10.

2. Julian, *Consolation upon the Departure of Sallust* 241C.

3. Julian, "To Evagrius."

4. Julian, *Hymn to Helios* 130C–D.

5. Julian, *Panegyric in Honor of Eusebia* 118.

CHAPTER 3. GAUL

1. Ammianus Marcellinus, *History* 25.4.

2. Julian, "To His Uncle Julian" no. 29.

3. Ammianus Marcellinus, *History* 16.10.

4. Julian, "To Himerius."

5. Julian, "To Eutherius."

6. Julian, *Consolation upon the Departure of Sallust* 240B.

7. Julian, *Panegyric in Honor of the Emperor Constantius* 11.

8. Julian, *Panegyric in Honor of the Emperor Constantius* 7D.

9. Julian, *Panegyric in Honor of the Emperor Constantius* 9A.

10. Sulpicius Severus, *The Life of Saint Martin* 4.

11. Julian, "To Priscus."

12. Quoted in George Kedrenos, *Synopsis of World History* (*Compendium Historiarum*), 532.

13. Julian, *The Heroic Deeds of Constantius* 50B.

CHAPTER 4. REBELLION

1. Julian, *Letter to the Senate and People of Athens* 270C.

CHAPTER 5. CONSTANTINOPLE

1. Julian, "To Maximus, the Philosopher."

2. Julian, "To Basil."

3. Julian, "To Bishop Aetius."

4. Julian, "To His Uncle Julian" no. 9.

5. Julian, *Letter to Themistius the Philosopher* 254A, 260B.

6. Libanius, "Funeral Oration over Julian," *Selected Orations* 18.130.

CHAPTER 6. AGAINST THE GALILEANS

1. Julian, "To Atarbius."

2. Ammianus Marcellinus, *History* 23.5.

3. Julian, "The Emperor Julian Caesar, Most Mighty Augustus, to the People of Alexandria."

4. Julian, "To Ecdicius, Prefect of Egypt" no. 23.

5. Julian, *To the Cynic Heracleios* 224B.

6. Julian, *To the Uneducated Cynics* 203B.

7. Julian, *Hymn to Helios* 130B.

8. Julian, *Hymn to Helios* 131B.

9. Julian, *Hymn to the Mother of the Gods* 166A, 161B.

10. Julian, "To Prohaeresius."

11. Julian, "To Ecdicius, Prefect of Egypt" no. 49.

12. Julian, "To Arsacius, High Priest of Galatia"; Julian, *Fragment of a Letter to a Priest* 305C.

13. Julian, *Fragment of a Letter to a Priest* 304C.

14. Julian, "To the Community of the Jews."

15. Ammianus Marcellinus, *History* 23.

16. Julian, "To the Alexandrians, an Edict."

17. Julian, "To Ecdicius, Prefect of Egypt" no. 46.

CHAPTER 7. ANTIOCH

1. Acts of the Apostles 11:26.

2. Julian, *Misopogon* 368C.

3. Julian, *Misopogon* 338A–B.

4. Julian, *Misopogon* 339B

5. Julian, *Misopogon* 339C.

6. Julian, *Misopogon* 340A.

7. Julian, *Misopogon* 370B.

8. Julian, *The Caesars* 336A–B.

9. Julian, *Against the Galileans* 39A.

10. Jerome, *Latin Commentary on Hosea* 3.11 (quotes Julian, Fragment 7: Against the Galileans.

11. Julian, *Against the Galileans* 39B.

12. Julian, *Against the Galileans* 89A.

CHAPTER 8. PERSIA

1. Julian, "To Libanius, Sophist and Quaestor."

2. Julian, "To Arsaces, Satrap of Armenia."

3. Ammianus Marcellinus, *History* 23.5.

4. Ammianus Marcellinus, *History* 24.7.

5. Gregory of Nazianus, *Orations* 5.10.

6. Ammianus Marcellinus, *History* 24.7.

7. Ammianus Marcellinus, *History* 25.3.23.

8. Julian, *Hymn to Helios* 158C.

CHAPTER 9. LEGACY

1. Ephrem *Hymns Against Julian* 3.1.

2. Zosimus, *History* 3.34.

3. Libanius, "The Lament over Julian," *Selected Orations* 17.7.

Bibliography

For the ancient Greek and Latin texts, I have used the editions of the Loeb Classical Library from Harvard University Press, which contain facing-page translations; in cases where there is no Loeb for a source I have listed a readily available English translation. All translations in the text are my own.

WORKS OF JULIAN AND OTHER ANCIENT SOURCES

Ammianus Marcellinus. *History.* Vol. 1: *Books 14–19.* Trans. John C. Rolfe. Loeb Classical Library 300. Cambridge: Harvard University Press, 1950. Vol. 2: *Books 20–26.* Trans. John. C. Rolfe. Loeb Classical Library 315. Cambridge: Harvard University Press, 1940.

Ephrem. *Hymns Against Julian.* In *Ephrem the Syrian: Hymns.* Trans. Kathleen E. McVey. Mahwah, N.J.: Paulist Press, 1989.

Gregory of Nazianus. *Orations.* In Saint Gregory of Nazianus, *Select Orations.* Trans. Martha Pollard Vinson. Fathers of the Church 107. Washington, D.C.: Catholic University of America Press, 2003.

Jerome. *Latin Commentary on Hosea.* In Jerome, *Commentaries on the Twelve Prophets.* Ancient Christian Texts 2. Trans. Thomas P. Scheck. Westmont, Ill.: InterVarsity Press, 2017.

Julian. *Works of the Emperor Julian.* Vol. 1: *Orations 1–5.* Trans. Wilmer C. Wright. Loeb Classical Library 13. Cambridge: Harvard University Press, 1913.

———. *Works of the Emperor Julian.* Vol. 2: *Orations 6–8. Letters to Themistius, To the Senate and People of Athens, To a Priest. The Caesars. Misopogon.* Trans. Wilmer C. Wright. Loeb Classical Library 29. Cambridge: Harvard University Press, 1913.

———. *Works of the Emperor Julian.* Vol. 3: *Letters. Epigrams. Against the Galileans. Fragments.* Trans. Wilmer C. Wright. Loeb Classical Library 157. Cambridge: Harvard University Press, 1923.

Against the Galileans (vol. 3)

The Caesars (vol. 2)

Consolation upon the Departure of Sallust (vol. 2)

"The Emperor Julian Caesar, Most Mighty Augustus, to the People of Alexandria," *Letters*, no. 21 (vol. 3)

Fragment of a Letter to a Priest (vol. 2)

Bibliography

The Heroic Deeds of Constantius (vol. 1)

Hymn to Helios (vol. 1)

Hymn to the Mother of the Gods (vol. 1)

Letter to Themistius the Philosopher (vol. 2)

Letter to the Senate and People of Athens (vol. 2)

Misopogon (vol. 2)

Panegyric in Honor of Eusebia (vol. 1)

Panegyric in Honor of the Emperor Constantius (vol. 1)

"To Arsaces, Satrap of Armenia," *Letters,* no. 57 (vol. 3)

"To Arsacius, High Priest of Galatia," *Letters,* no. 22 (vol. 3)

"To Atarbius," *Letters,* no. 37 (vol. 3)

"To Basil," *Letters,* no. 26 (vol. 3)

"To Bishop Aetius," *Letters,* no. 15 (vol. 3)

"To Ecdicius, Prefect of Egypt," *Letters,* nos. 23, 46, 49 (vol. 3)

"To Eutherius," *Letters,* no. 10 (vol. 3)

"To Evagrius," *Letters,* no. 25 (vol. 3)

"To Himerius," *Letters,* no. 69 (vol. 3)

"To His Uncle Julian," *Letters,* nos. 9, 29 (vol. 3)

"To Libanius, Sophist and Quaestor," *Letters,* no. 58 (vol. 3)

"To Maximus, the Philosopher," *Letters,* no. 8 (vol. 3)

"To Priscus," *Letters,* no. 1 (vol. 3)

"To Prohaeresius," *Letters,* no. 14 (vol. 3)

"To the Alexandrians, an Edict," *Letters,* no. 24 (vol. 3)

"To the Community of the Jews," *Letters,* no. 51 (vol. 3)

To the Cynic Heracleios (vol. 2)

To the Uneducated Cynics (vol. 2)

Libanius. *Selected Orations.* Vol. 1. Trans. A. F. Norman. Loeb Classical Library 451. Cambridge: Harvard University Press, 1969.

Pliny the Younger. *Letters, Books 8–10, Panegyricus.* Trans. Betty Radice. Loeb Classical Library 59. Cambridge: Harvard University Press, 1969.

Bibliography

Sulpicius Severus. *The Life of Saint Martin.* In Sulpicius Severus, *The Complete Works.* Trans. Richard J. Goodrich. New York: Newman Press, 2015.

Zosimus. *History.* In Zosimus, *New History.* Trans. Ronald T. Ridley. Leiden: Brill, 2017.

MODERN SOURCES

Bowersock, G. W. *Julian the Apostate.* Cambridge: Harvard University Press, 1978.

Murdoch, Adrian. *The Last Pagan: Julian the Apostate and the Death of the Ancient World.* Rochester, Vt.: Inner Traditions, 2008.

Rebenich, Stefan, and Hans-Ulrich Wiemar, eds. *A Companion to Julian the Apostate.* Leiden: Brill, 2020.

Teitler, H. C. *The Last Pagan Emperor: Julian the Apostate and the War Against Christianity.* Oxford: Oxford University Press, 2017.

Index

Index

Index

Index

Ephrem (Christian historian), 7, 130
Eunapius, 7
Euphrates River, 115–116, 118–119
Eusebia (wife of Constantius), 36–38, 41
Eusebius (Arian bishop), 25–27
Eusebius (imperial court eunuch), 36, 79
Eusebius (of Myndus; philosopher),
    33–34
Eutherius, 44–45

Fausta (wife of Constantine), 15, 42
Florentius, 66, 67, 79
Franks, 1, 15, 47, 57–58, 65

Galen, 59
Galerius (Roman emperor), 14–15, 120
Galileans (Julian's term for Christians),
    74, 85–87, 89, 95
Galla (first wife of Julius Constantius),
    24
Gallus (emperor, half-brother of Julian):
    Anomoeans and, 74; Apollo's Tem-
    ple at Daphne and, 105; Barbatio
    and, 53; elevated to Caesar by
    Constantius, 32, 35; executed by
    Constantius, 35–36, 53; exiled
    to Macellum, 27–28; fighting in
    Persia, 32, 35; half-brother to Julian,
    24, 28; marriage to Constantia,
    39–40; meeting with Constantius,
    24; military and administrative
    training of, 30; punishment of
    those responsible for downfall
    of, 79
Gaul, 1–2, 42–60; Autun as Julian's first
    military victory in, 50; Constantius
    (Chlorus) defending for Rome,
    12–13; Constantius-Julian relations
    during Julian's time in, 43–44,
    52–53, 57, 62, 64–65; Eutherius's
    role in, 44–45; Germanic tribes as
    threat to, 1–2, 13–15, 32, 37, 42–43,

47, 51–53, 65; Julian and his troops
    in Paris, 62–63; Julian assigned to,
    1–2, 38, 42; Julian's success as mili-
    tary leader in, 53–58, 60; Marcellus
    in, 51–53; pagan majority in, 46–47;
    Roman annexation of, 42; Salutius's
    role in, 45–46; Strasbourg, Battle
    of, 53–58; Vadomar's role against
    Julian in, 66–67; winter camps/
    headquarters of Romans, 51–52,
    58, 65. See also Alamanni; Franks;
    Germanic tribes
George (bishop of Cappadocia), 29–30,
    87–88
Germanic tribes: Christian conversion
    of, 20, 42; Constantius recruiting
    against Magnentius, 43; as threat
    to Roman Gaul, 1–2, 13–15, 32, 37,
    42–43, 47, 49–53, 65. See also
    Alamanni
Gibbon, Edward, Decline and Fall of the
    Roman Empire, 132
gods, worship of. See pagan worship
Gordian III (Roman emperor), 119
Gratian (Christian Roman emperor),
    131
Greco-Roman worship. See pagan wor-
    ship; and specific gods and goddesses
Gregory of Nazianzus, 6, 28, 31, 34, 123

Hadrian's Wall, 13
Hecate (Greco-Roman goddess), 34
Hecebolius, 30, 31
Helena (mother of Constantine the
    Great), 13, 21, 103
Helena (wife of Julian), 39–42, 127
Helios (Greco-Roman god), 28; Julian's
    hymn to, 91–92, 126
Hellenism, 26, 73, 74, 96
Hierapolis, 116
Himerius, 41
Homer, Iliad, 60

Index

Iamblichus, 32

Illyricum, 66–68. *See also* Nish

imperial court, evolution of, 80

Jerusalem, sack of Jewish Temple and possibility of rebuilding in, 98–99

Jesus Christ: *Against the Galileans* as refutation of, 108–110; Anomoeans' views on, 74; Arian dispute over nature of, 19–21, 25; Chi-Rho as symbol of, 16, 114; Council of Nicaea on nature of, 20–21; on hypocrisy, 93; on the poor as inheriting kingdom of heaven, 100; prophecy on Jewish Temple in Jerusalem, 97–98; Roman views at time of crucifixion, 10. *See also* Christianity and Christians

Jews and Judaism, 3–4, 17, 33, 35, 86, 97–99, 101, 109

John Chrysostom, 31

Jovian (Flavius Jovianus, cavalry commander, later emperor), 67–68, 78, 128–130

Julian (Flavius Claudius Julianus): appearance of, 39, 72; in Athens, 34–35; as Augustus, by army proclamation, 2, 63, 65–66; birth of, 9, 24; at Bithynia, 25–27; as Caesar, 1–2, 38, 44, 51, 57, 64, 65–66; called Julian the Apostate, 3–4, 132; childhood and education of, 23–30; as co-consul with Constantius, 47, 52, 66; in Constantinople for further studies, 30; contemporary commentators on, 5–6; death of, 4, 126–127; in Ephesus, 34–35; exiled to Macellum, 27–30, 87; exiled to Nicomedia, 31; family background and genealogy, 13, 48, 137; first military victory of, 50; funeral and inscription on tomb, 6, 130; Gallus's

execution's effect on, 35–36; in Gaul, 1–2, 42–60; legacy of, 132–133; marriage to Helena, 39–42, 127; meeting with Constantius, 24; military prowess, 4, 44, 97, 113; oratory skills, 55; in Pergamum, 32, 33–34; recalled by Constantius, 36–38; removal of his remains to Church of the Holy Apostles, 131; as scholar, 29–32, 36, 43, 73, 88; sources on, 4–7; spared from Constantius's killing of family members, 2, 24; temperament, 39–42, 44, 79–80, 96; tomb in Tarsus, 130. *See also* Christianity and Christians; Gaul; pagan worship; Persian campaign by Julian; rebellion

— as emperor: in Antioch, 102–111; appeals of city and town grievances heard by, 83; armies declaring loyalty to, 76, 77; assassination threats against, 115; beard worn by, 72, 106; Constantinople as imperial capital of, 73, 76–84; corruption targeted by, 81–83; courier system changes by, 82; funeral of Constantius as show of respect from, 76–77; golden wreath offerings no longer required by, 82–83; governance and bureaucracy reforms of, 81–84; imperial court changes by, 80–81; imperial decrees by, 7, 82, 86; letters written upon assuming throne, 73–76; military tribunals in Chalcedon organized by, 76–79; oracle predicting short reign for, 94; revoking exile of those banished by Constantius, 74; setting Christian factions against each other, 74–75; succeeding to throne upon Constantius's death, 3, 70, 71; successor to, difficulty in choosing, 127–128;

Index

Index